WHAT YOUR
FIRST GRADER
NEEDS
TO KNOW

THE CORE KNOWLEDGE SERIES

RESOURCE BOOKS FOR GRADES ONE THROUGH SIX
BOOK I

DOUBLEDAY

New York London Toronto Sydney Auckland

THE·CORE·KNOWLEDGE
SERIES

WHAT YOUR FIRST GRADER NEEDS TO KNOW

FUNDAMENTALS OF A GOOD FIRST-GRADE EDUCATION

Edited by

E. D. HIRSCH, JR.

PUBLISHED BY DOUBLEDAY

a division of Bantam Doubleday Dell Publishing Group, Inc.
1540 Broadway, New York, New York 10036

DOUBLEDAY and the portrayal of an anchor with a dolphin are trademarks of Doubleday, a division of
Bantam Doubleday Dell Publishing Group, Inc.

Library of Congress Cataloging-in-Publication Data
What your first grader needs to know / edited by E. D. Hirsch, Jr. — 1st
  ed.
    p.   cm. — (The core knowledge series; bk. 1)
  Includes bibliographical references and index.
  1. First grade (Education)—United States.   2. Curriculum
planning—United States.   I. Hirsch, E. D. (Eric Donald), 1928–
II. Series.
LB1571   1st.W53   1991
372.19—dc20   90-26141
                                                       CIP

ISBN 0-385-41115-4

20   19   18   17   16

This book is dedicated to the memory of
Paul Bell
late superintendent of Dade County Public Schools

"Because he kept the Divine Vision in time of trouble."
(William Blake, *Jerusalem*, II:30)

Acknowledgments

This series has depended upon the help, advice, and encouragement of some two thousand people. Some of those singled out here know already the depth of my gratitude; others may be surprised to find themselves thanked publicly for help they gave quietly and freely for the sake of the enterprise alone. To helpers named and unnamed I am deeply grateful.

Project Manager: Tricia Emlet

Editors: Tricia Emlet (Text), Rae Grant (Art)

Artists and Writers: Nancy Bryson (Physical Science), Tricia Emlet (Sayings), Leslie Evans (Artwork), Jonathan Fuqua (Artwork), Julie C. Grant (Artwork), Marie Hawthorne (Science Biographies), John Hirsch (Mathematics), Pamela C. Johnson (History & Geography), Blair Logwood Jones (Literature), Gail Macintosh (Artwork), A. Brooke Russell (Life Science), Peter Ryan (Fine Arts & Mythology), Lindley Shutz (Language & Literature), Giuseppe Trogu (Artwork), James D. Watkinson (History & Geography)

Art and Photo Research: Rae Grant

Research Assistants: Candice Bredbenner (Illustrations), Martha Clay (Permissions), Paige Turner (Text)

Advisers on Multiculturalism: Minerva Allen, Frank de Varona, Mick Fedullo, Dorothy Fields, Elizabeth Fox-Genovese, Marcia Galli, Dan Garner, Henry Louis Gates, Cheryl Kulas, Joseph C. Miller, Gerry Raining Bird, Dorothy Small, Sharon Stewart-Peregoy, Sterling Stuckey, Marlene Walking Bear, Lucille Watahomigie, Ramona Wilson

Advisers on Elementary Education: Joseph Adelson, Isobel Beck, Paul Bell, Carl Bereiter, David Bjorklund, Constance Jones, Elizabeth LaFuze, J. P. Lutz, Jean Osborne, Sandra Scarr, Nancy Stein, Phyllis Wilkin

Advisers on Technical Subject Matters: Richard Anderson, Andrew Gleason, Joseph Kett, Ralph Smith, Nancy Summers, James Trefil

Conferees, March 1990: Nola Bacci, Joan Baratz-Snowden, Thomasyne Beverley, Thomas Blackton, Angela Burkhalter, Monty Caldwell, Thomas M. Carroll, Laura Chapman, Carol Anne Collins, Lou Corsaro, Anne Coughlin, Henry Cotton, Arletta Dimberg, Debra P. Douglas,

Patricia Edwards, Janet Elenbogen, Mick Fedullo, Michele Fomalont, Nancy Gercke, Mamon Gibson, Jean Haines, Barbara Hayes, Stephen Herzog, Helen Kelley, Brenda King, John King, Elizabeth LaFuze, Diana Lam, Nancy Lambert, Doris Langaster, Richard LaPointe, Lloyd Leverton, Madeleine Long, Allen Luster, Joseph McGeehan, Janet McLin, Gloria McPhee, Marcia Mallard, Judith Matz, William J. Moloney, John Morabito, Robert Morrill, Roberta Morse, Karen Nathan, Dawn Nichols, Valeta Paige, Mary Perrin, Joseph Piazza, Jeanne Price, Marilyn Rauth, Judith Raybern, Mary Reese, Richard Rice, Wallace Saval, John Saxon, Jan Schwab, Ted Sharp, Diana Smith, Richard Smith, Trevanian Smith, Carol Stevens, Nancy Summers, Michael Terry, Robert Todd, Elois Veltman, Sharon Walker, Mary Ann Ward, Penny Williams, Charles Wootten, Clarke Worthington, Jane York

The Three Oaks Elementary School: Constance Jones, Principal; Cecelia Cook, Assistant Principal

Teachers: Joanne Anderson, Linda Anderson, Nancy Annichiarico, Deborah Backes, Katherine Ann Bedingfield, Barbara Bittner, Michael Blue, Coral Boudin, Nancy Bulgerin, Jodene Cebak, Cheryl Chastain, Paula Clark, Betty Cook, Laura DeProfio, Holly DeSantis, Cindy Donmoyer, Lisa Eastridge, Amy Germer, Elizabeth Graves, Jennifer Gunder, Eileen Hafer, Helen Hallman, Donna Hernandez, Kathleen Holzborn, Robert Horner, Jenni Jones, Zoe Ann Klusacek, Annette Lopez, Barbara Lyon, Cindy Miller, Lelar Miller, Laura Morse, Karen Naylor, Joanne O'Neill, Jill Pearson, Linda Peck, Rebecca Poppe, Janet Posch, Judy Quest, Angie Richards, Angie Ryan, April Santarelli, Patricia Scott, Patricia Stapleton, Pamela Stewart, Jeanne Storm, Phillip Storm, Katherine Twomey, Karen Ward

Benefactors: the Dade County School District, the Exxon Education Foundation, the Lee County School District, the National Endowment for the Humanities, the Richmond Newspapers, the Shutz Foundation

Morale Boosters: Polly Hirsch, Robert Payton, Rafe Sagalyn.

Our grateful acknowledgment to these persons does not imply that we have taken their (sometimes conflicting) advice in every case, or that each of them endorses all aspects of this project. Responsibility for final decisions must rest with the editor alone. Suggestions for improvements are very welcome, and I wish to thank in advance those who send advice for revising and improving this series.

Contents

Acknowledgments   viii
General Introduction   1
How to Use This Book—For Parents and Teachers   11

I. LANGUAGE ARTS

Introduction to Familiar Rhymes and Stories—*For Parents
  and Teachers*   14

About Stories and Poems   16
  Who Was Mother Goose?   16
Familiar Rhymes   17
  A Diller, a Dollar   17
  Early to Bed   17
  Baa, Baa, Black Sheep   17
  Diddle, Diddle, Dumpling   17
  Jack Sprat   17
  Ladybug, Ladybug   17
  Georgie Porgie   18
  Hey, Diddle, Diddle   18
  Jack and Jill   18
  Hickory, Dickory, Dock   18
  Hot Cross Buns!   18
  Here We Go Round the Mulberry Bush   19
  London Bridge Is Falling Down   19
  Humpty Dumpty   19
  Little Boy Blue   19
  Jack Be Nimble   19
  Mary, Mary, Quite Contrary   20
  Mary Had a Little Lamb   20
  Little Miss Muffet   20
  Old King Cole   20
  Little Bo Peep   21
  One, Two, Buckle My Shoe   21
  Little Jack Horner   21
  Pat-a-Cake   21
  Ring Around the Rosey   21

The Owl and the Pussycat   22
Old Mother Hubbard   23
Star Light, Star Bright   23
Ride a Cock-horse   23
Tom, Tom, the Piper's Son   23
See-Saw, Margery Daw   23
Rock-a-bye, Baby   23
Rub-a-dub-dub   24
Rain, Rain, Go Away   24
Sing a Song of Sixpence   24
Roses Are Red   24
There Was a Little Girl   25
Three Blind Mice   25
Twinkle, Twinkle, Little Star   25
Simple Simon   25
There Was an Old Woman Who Lived in a Shoe   26
This Little Pig Went to Market   26
Stories   27
Anansi Rides Tiger   27
Chicken Little   28
Cinderella   29
Goldilocks and the Three Bears   31
Jack and the Beanstalk   32
The Little Red Hen   34
Little Red Riding Hood   35
Medio Pollito   37
Peter Rabbit   38
The Pied Piper of Hamelin   40
Pinocchio   42
The Princess and the Pea   43
Puss-in-Boots   44
Rapunzel   46
Rumpelstiltskin   48
Sleeping Beauty   50
Snow White   52
The Three Little Pigs   54
The Ugly Duckling   55
Why the Owl Has Big Eyes   56
What Are Fables?   58
From Aesop's Fables   59
The Boy Who Cried Wolf   59
The Dog in the Manger   60
The Wolf in Sheep's Clothing   60
The Maid and the Milk Pail   61
The Fox and the Grapes   62
The Hare and the Tortoise   62
The Goose and the Golden Eggs   63

Myths and Other Stories 64
   Myths and Legends 64
   Fairies, Elves, Leprechauns, Trolls 64
   A Troll Story: The Three Billy Goats Gruff 65
   The Legend of Oedipus and the Sphinx 66
   The Legend of the Minotaur, Daedalus, and Icarus 67
   The Fable of Brer Rabbit and the Tar Baby 68

Introduction to Language and Literature—*For Parents and Teachers* 70
Learning About Language 71
   Words and Letters 71
   Small Letters and Capital Letters 72
   The Letter S 73
   Sentences and Paragraphs 73
   Punctuation Marks 73
Learning About Literature 75
   Prose and Rhyme 75
   Heroes and Heroines and Other Characters 76

Introduction to Sayings—*For Parents and Teachers* 77
Sayings and Phrases 78
   A.M. and P.M. 78
   An apple a day keeps the doctor away 78
   April showers bring May flowers 79
   Do unto others as you would have them do unto you 79
   Fish out of water 79
   Hit the nail on the head 79
   If at first you don't succeed, try, try again 80
   Let the cat out of the bag 80
   The more the merrier 80
   Never leave till tomorrow what you can do today 80
   Practice makes perfect 81
   Raining cats and dogs 81
   There's no place like home 81

II. GEOGRAPHY, WORLD CIVILIZATION, AND AMERICAN CIVILIZATION

Introduction to Geography—*For Parents and Teachers* 84
Geography 86
The Earth: A Huge Ball 86
A Map of the World 86
   How to Look at a Map 87
   Oceans 88

Land	88
The Equator	88
The Continents	89
Asia	89
Europe	90
Africa	91
North America	92
Canada	93
United States	94
Mexico and Central America	94
South America	95
Antarctica	95
Australia	96
Introduction to World Civilization—*For Parents and Teachers*	97
World Civilization	99
Everybody's Story	99
The Nile Gives Tut a Present	99
The First Kingdom	101
What Are Mummies?	103
Animal Gods	104
Babylonia: Another Gift	105
Judaism	105
Christianity	106
Islam	107
Hinduism	107
Buddha: A Young Prince	107
Buddha Stops an Elephant	108
Confucius: A Poor Chinese Boy	108
Happy New Year	109
Introduction to American Civilization—*For Parents and Teachers*	111
American Civilization	112
Legends and Leaders	112
Who Built the Bridge?	112
A Very Long Trip	112
Cities in the Jungle: The Maya	114
City on the Lake: The Aztecs	115
Cities in the Clouds: The Incas	116
The Big Surprise	116
Columbus Finds a New World	117

Horses and Guns	118
Smallpox	118
Cortés: The Aztecs Lose	119
Pizarro: The Incas Lose	119
The U.S.A.: Good-for-Nothing Lands	120
Good Lands	120
England Enters	120
The Lost Colony	122
Jamestown and the People of Pocahontas	122
Pilgrims	123
The Puritans	124
Thirteen Colonies	125
A Trail Blazer	126
Slavery	126
The King's Mistake	127
A Tea Party	127
A Famous Man	128
A Shot Heard Round the World	129
Birthday	130
Liberty Bell	131
Freedom for All?	131
Two Women	132
Two Freed Women	132
A Father	133
A Cherry Tree	133
Twice as Big	134
The Fight Goes On	135
Sequoyah	136
What's Left?	136

III. FINE ARTS

Introduction to the Fine Arts—*For Parents and Teachers*	138
The Fine Arts	139
Literature	139
Music	140
Row, Row, Row Your Boat	140
London Bridge Is Falling Down	140
Yankee Doodle	141

Hush, Little Baby   141
Here We Go Round the Mulberry Bush   141
The Star-Spangled Banner   142
Vocal and Instrumental Music   142
The Many Different Kinds of Music   143
Folk Music   143
Down in the Valley   143
I've Been Working on the Railroad   144
Classical Music   144
Twinkle, Twinkle, Little Star   145
Jazz   146
When the Saints Go Marching In   146
Louis Armstrong   147
The Three Parts of Music: Melody, Rhythm, and Harmony   147
Melody   148
Oh, Susanna!   148
America the Beautiful   148
Rhythm   149
Pat-a-Cake   149
Harmony   150
Dance   150
Folk Dancing   151
Ballet   151
Tap Dancing   152
Art   152
Art Is Found in All Times and Places   152
Symmetry and Patterns in Arts and Crafts   153
Portraits   154
Architecture and Sculpture   155

IV. MATHEMATICS

Introduction to Mathematics—Grades One Through Six—
For Parents and Teachers   158
Introduction to First-Grade Mathematics—*For Parents and
Teachers*   160
First-Grade Mathematics   161
Numbers from 0 to 10   161
Working with the Numbers Up to 10   163
Addition   163
Greater Than and Less Than   168
Subtraction   170

Fact Families 173
Ordinal Numbers 175
Place Value 175
Arithmetic and Calculators 178
Geometry 179
Fractions 182
Telling Time 183
The Calendar 186
More Addition and Subtraction 187
Counting Money 191
Math Stories 194

V. NATURAL SCIENCES

Introduction to Life Sciences—*For Parents and Teachers* 196
Life Sciences 198
Plants and Animals 198
The World of Plants 199
Deciduous and Evergreen Plants 200
Flowers and Seeds 200
Animals 201
The Food Chain 202
Habitats 203
Air and Treetop Habitats 203
Forest Habitats 204
Meadow and Prairie Habitats 204
Water Habitats 204
Desert Habitats 205
Underground Habitats 205
Habitat Destruction 206
Special Types of Animals 207
Extinct Animals 207
Wild and Domestic Animals 207
Pets 207
A Very Special Animal—You 208
Your Body 208
Taking Care of Your Body 210

Introduction to Physical Sciences—*For Parents and Teachers* 212
Physical Sciences 214
Measurement 214

Length   216
Matter   217
Volume   218
Temperature and Thermometer   219
Time   220
The Earth   221
    The Earth's Surface   222
    Inside the Earth   223
    Weather and the Earth's Atmosphere   224
The Moon   225
The Sun and Energy, Part One   226
The Sun and Energy, Part Two   228
Experiments   228
Stories of Scientists   231
    Nicolaus Copernicus   231
    Charles Drew   232
    Rachel Carson   233

Illustration and Photo Credits   237
Index   239

WHAT YOUR FIRST GRADER NEEDS TO KNOW

General Introduction

I. The Critical Early Grades

In 1987 I published a book, *Cultural Literacy*, that described the decline of American education over the past four decades, and offered suggestions for reversing that decline. Though sprinkled with scholarly footnotes and descriptions of research, the book, to everyone's surprise, became a best-seller. Hundreds of supporting letters from parents and teachers inspired me to set up a foundation devoted to the educational improvements that *Cultural Literacy* advocated. For the past four years, that organization, the Core Knowledge Foundation, has sought and gained the help of some two thousand teachers and scholars in focusing on a single education reform: imparting a core of shared knowledge to all elementary school students from first through sixth grade. The present series is the first fruit of that cooperative, nationwide effort.

After a long process of consultation and consensus building (which I shall describe in a moment) agreement was reached on a specific sequence of core knowledge that young Americans should, at a minimum, learn. That is the knowledge sequence upon which this series of books is based. The sequence itself is freely available to all publishers and educators through the Core Knowledge Foundation. Our hope is that this sequence, duly revised over time, will gradually come to be accepted, and that publishers, schools, parents, and educators will join in the cause of promoting shared knowledge in the elementary school years.

This core sequence is not meant to be the whole of the school curriculum, nor is the information narrated in this series meant to be constantly stressed above other forms of knowledge and skill. Teaching a common core of knowledge can coexist with a great diversity of instructional methods, emphases, and additional subject matters. In fact, parents' or teachers' confidence that a core of essential knowledge has been imparted to children allows them a freer rein to encourage variety, imagination, and inventiveness in education, as well as to cultivate the special character of the child, the home, the school, or community. In this period of our national life, to ensure that all young children possess a core of shared knowledge is a fundamental reform that, while not sufficient by itself to achieve excellence and fairness in schooling, is nonetheless a *necessary* step in developing a first-rate educational system in the United States.

The weakest link in the chain of our public education is elementary school—grades one through six. Although the usual evidence that we are "a nation at risk" comes from achievement tests that are taken in grades seven and twelve, the poor performance of American students in those grades can be traced directly to shortcomings inherited from elementary schools that have not systematically imparted the knowledge students need for further learning. Poor early preparation hinders many unfortunate students from learning what is *in* the seven-through-twelve curriculum, while fortunate ones are enabled to learn only by having gained needed background knowledge outside school. The inequitable result, surprising for a nation built upon ideals of equality, is that our public educational system is the least *fair* system in the developed world. Because knowledge builds upon knowledge, the differences between our academic haves and have-nots increase dramatically as our students advance through the elementary grades, until, by the time of junior high school, many knowledge-deprived students of high native ability are put into special "low-ability tracks" where the deprivation is further compounded. Small wonder that the comparative performance of American public education, poor by all standards, is worst by the standard of fairness.

II. Why Core Knowledge Is Needed

A core of shared knowledge in elementary grades is necessary for excellence and fairness in schooling. Before I outline the reasons for making this blunt assertion, I shall briefly mention a striking piece of evidence which supports it. All of the best—i.e., highest-achieving and most egalitarian—elementary school systems in the world, such as those in Sweden, France, and Japan, teach their children a specific core of knowledge in each of the first six grades, thus enabling all children to enter each new grade with a secure foundation for further learning. By contrast, those educational systems that have recently declined in educational achievement, England, Australia, and the United States, did *not* give children a specific core of shared knowledge in early grades. Research could have predicted that result for reasons that are apparent to common sense. Here they are, briefly.

(1) Shared background knowledge makes schooling more effective. The one-on-one tutorial is the most effective form of schooling, in part because a parent or teacher is able to provide tailor-made instruction for the individual child. The tutor knows what the child already knows, and can build upon that already-acquired knowledge to teach something new. In a nontutorial situation, say, in a classroom of twenty-five students, one cannot effectively build new knowledge for all students unless they all share the background knowledge that is being built upon. When all the students in a class *do* share that relevant background knowledge, a classroom can begin to approach the effectiveness of a tutorial.

(2) Shared background knowledge makes schooling more fair and democratic. When all the children who enter a grade can be assumed to share some of the same building blocks of knowledge, and when the teacher knows exactly what those building blocks are, then all students are empowered to learn. Even when some children in a class don't have elements of the core knowledge they were supposed to acquire in previous grades, the possibility of identifying exactly what the knowledge gaps are enables the teacher or parent greatly to speed up the process of making up for lost time, giving all students a chance to fulfill their potentials in later grades. Under a core-knowledge system, by the same token, students who have to move from school to school are treated more fairly. When they enter a new school they are on a more equal footing with their classmates than are students in a system like ours. For these reasons, school systems that use core standards have proved to be more democratic and fair than systems like ours which do not.

(3) Defining a specific core of knowledge for each grade motivates everyone through definite, attainable standards. This is not the place to discuss the great political issue of making schools accountable for their outcomes by defining more concretely the goals that are to be achieved. On the other hand, accountability in education is important and motivational for children themselves. Children who are made aware of clearly defined, achievable learning goals can monitor and take pleasure in their progress. Attainment of those defined goals should be expected, demanded, and when achieved, praised. The self-esteem of children, so important for their later confidence and ambition, arises from *earned* self-esteem, not from praise that is automatically handed out on a regular basis regardless of accomplishment.

(4) Shared background knowledge helps create cooperation and solidarity in school and in the nation. The shared background knowledge that makes for communication and learning in academic work also makes for cooperation and toleration among students within the classroom community. In our diverse nation, students in a classroom usually come from varied home cultures, and those different cultures should be honored and understood by all students as part of the common core. Schooling should create a *school-based culture* that is common to all and welcoming to all because it includes knowledge of many cultures. Such shared, multicultural knowledge gives all our students, no matter what their background, a common ground for understanding our uncommon diversity.

The schools of a modern nation are the institutions through which children become members of the wider national community. They will grow to adults who will live cooperatively and sustain one another only if they feel that they truly *belong* to the larger society. Such universal belonging has always been the hope and promise of the United States. As the great American writer Herman Melville said in 1849: "We are not a narrow tribe.—No: our blood is as the flood of the Amazon, made up of a thousand noble currents all pouring into one. We are not a nation so much as a world." Here, above all, shared, school-based knowledge, which alone can lead to educational and social fairness, should be encouraged as part of our best traditions.

The evidence of educational decline and widening social unfairness has become ever more obvious and undeniable since my book was published in 1987. Verbal aptitude scores have dropped further. These declines are commonly explained by claiming that they arise from our democratic progress in bringing minorities into the school system. Alas, it is not true; the greatest decline has been in the numbers of students who make *high* scores. Worst of all, our fall from our own achievements seems even steeper when we compare our current situation with the educational advances made by other developed countries. They have moved forward as we have retreated. In 1970, American elementary students ranked seventh in science achievement among the seventeen countries measured. By 1980, we ranked fifteenth—third from bottom, just above the Philippines. That decline can be reversed. But no modern nation has achieved both excellence and fairness in education without defining core knowledge for the elementary school. It is reasonable to predict that we will fail to reverse our educational decline unless we do the same.

III. The Core Knowledge Sequence: How Consensus Was Achieved

The first question that many Americans ask of those who advocate a core sequence in elementary school is: *"Who decides what the core will be?"* That difficult question, so admirable and so American in its suspicion of central authority, has caused many to conclude that the subject of core standards is best left alone. In democracies like Sweden, Japan, and France, the question "Who decides?" has the following answer: "A central ministry of education that is accountable to the national legislature." But American traditions go strongly against such an arrangement, even though historians have shown that a common elementary school core was achieved informally in earlier periods of our history through an unspoken agreement among a small group of educational publishers in New York and New England. In the past forty years that unspoken agreement has vanished.

Sensing the need for a common sequence, the National Council of Teachers of Mathematics, the American Association for the Advancement of Science, and other professional organizations as well as state departments of education have begun to recommend general outcomes for elementary and secondary education. The recent reports that these organizations have produced are useful as general guides, but are not specific enough to induce the teaching of a common core of knowledge in a common sequence. My colleagues and I have therefore used their recommendations as starting points, and have further amplified them in order to reach consensus on a definite sequence.

First, we analyzed the knowledge and skills that the reports recommended. We also tabulated the knowledge and skills through grade six that were defined in several successful educational systems of other countries, including France, Japan, Sweden, and West Germany. In addition, we formed an advisory board on multiculturalism that reached agreements about the core knowledge of diverse cultural traditions that American children should share as part of their school-based common culture. We sent all these materials to three independent groups of teachers, scholars, and scientists around the country asking them to create a master list of the core knowledge children should have by the end of grade six. About 150 teachers (including college teachers), scientists, and administrators were involved in this initial step.

These items were amalgamated into a master list, and further groups of teachers and specialists were asked to agree on a grade-by-grade sequence of the list. That sequence was sent in turn to some one hundred educators and specialists who participated in a national conference called to hammer out a definite agreement. This important meeting took place in March 1990. The conferees were elementary school teachers, curriculum specialists, scientists, science writers, officers of national organizations, representatives of ethnic groups, district superintendents, and school principals from every region of the country. A total of twenty-four working groups decided on revisions in the sequence, and these revisions were presented to plenary sessions, where they were accepted or rejected by majority vote. The sequence that ultimately came out of the conference was fine-tuned during the 1990–91 academic year at the Three Oaks Elementary School in Lee County, Florida.

Thus was the sequence agreed upon that forms the basis for this series. In the United States, each school and district decides its own curriculum. But there is growing recognition that students will greatly benefit if *part* of that curriculum includes a sequence of core-knowledge goals that are pursued throughout the nation. Whether the core sequence that is finally agreed upon will be based on the one that is presented here cannot be known; perhaps some other group will bring forward a sequence that is a more attractive candidate for public acceptance. But whatever sequence is chosen, we can be sure that the answer to the question, "Who decides?" will ultimately be, as always in a democracy, "The people decide."

IV. The Nature of This Series

The *Core Knowledge Series* is a grade-by-grade presentation of the knowledge young people should acquire in early grades. The books have been sequenced to help children make secure progress in learning; each book presents knowledge upon which later books will build. Our writers have drawn on their experience and common sense to make the materials interesting, clear, and challenging. We have *not* used discredited grade-level formulas regarding vocabulary and sentence length. Instead, we have gone to the source; drafts of the materials have been revised on the basis of teachers' actual experiences with children at the Three Oaks Elementary School.

Although we have made these books as good and useful as we can, parents and teachers should understand that they are not the only means by which the core-knowledge sequence can be imparted. The books represent a first step in the core-knowledge reform effort—a single version of the possibilities inherent in the core-knowledge sequence. We hope that publishers will be stimulated to offer educational videos, computer programs, games, alternative books, and a variety of imaginative vehicles based on the core-knowledge sequence.

The books are designed to be useful tools for parents and teachers, both at home and in school. They are called "resources" to signal that they neither replace the regular local school curriculum, nor provide everything that parents should impart to their children. The books are strategic instruments designed to help children gain some of the knowledge they will need to make progress in school and be effective in society.

Each book is divided into five main sections: language arts, social studies, fine arts, mathematics, and science. The main sections are further divided into subsections. It is a good idea for parents or teachers to read from two different main sections whenever they read aloud, in order to provide variety, and to help children make connections between domains. There is no one right way to combine the readings; indeed, there are numerous good ways.

During the school year, children go to classes in the United States an average of 180 days. In that time, using just twenty minutes a day, a parent or teacher could read aloud and discuss everything in Book I three times over. Excluding the math parts of these books, which take special practice, every child who is not learning-disabled could be on very familiar terms with everything in that book, by being read aloud to just a few minutes a day during school days.

If it's so easy for children to become familiar with core knowledge, and if children *like* to be informed about the world, why do our children tend to know so little about the sorts of things narrated in these books? Part of the answer is that the "basal readers" that our children are given to develop their reading skills tend to be content-poor books conveying little that is of value for later learning. American children spend so much time in early grades nourishing the skills of reading upon thin gruel that they haven't very much time left to gain significant knowledge.

Observing this, some experienced teachers have asked, "Why not teach reading *and* systematically impart knowledge at the same time?" To give parents and teachers that additional option is one purpose of this series. What young children learn should not be limited to what they can read for themselves. Most of what they learn should come from what they hear and observe when they are *not* focusing their minds on sounding out letters and words.

The act of listening to someone read is an important part of early learning. It makes the world of books familiar to children, and it increases their knowledge of words and things. In almost all children who reach the end of seventh grade, the ability to read and the ability to listen have reached exactly the same level. Thus, if a child in early grades knows a lot and can listen well, that same child will normally be reading well in later grades. And the opposite is true. If a child in early grades does not know very much, and cannot listen with much understanding, he or she will tend to be a poor reader later on. In the end, it is children's knowledge and their consequent ability to understand what books say that determines how skillful they will become at reading and learning.

Teachers and parents who use these books should remember that nothing can take the place of good teaching and parenting. The need for interactive, hands-on activities and patient practice is obvious in the sections on mathematics, the fine arts, and the natural sciences. The language of books must be supplemented for young children, to whom these books will serve mainly as sources of interesting stories and pictures. For parents and teachers, they will serve mainly as helps and guides. The books modestly announce themselves to be resources. We hope that they will serve their function usefully and well.

V. What You Can Do

The processes of education are so complex that almost any good educational idea, pursued single-mindedly or exclusively, will lead to failure. Unfortunately, one single point of view has dominated American elementary education over the past forty years, and a principal reason for the failure of our schools has been the elevation of a single set of insights to the level of universal truths. "Education should shun rote learning and encourage understanding." "Students should not be stuffed with mere facts (which are constantly changing), but should learn *how* to learn." "The child, not the academic subject, is the true focus of education." "Do not impose knowledge on children before they are developmentally ready to receive it." "Do not bog children down in mere facts, but rather, inculcate critical-thinking skills."

Who has not heard these sentiments, so admirable and humane, and so true—up to a point? But these positive sentiments in favor of developing a child's understanding are also expressed as negative sentiments *against* such practices as "rote learning" and a concern for "mere facts." By taking this strong negative stand against imparting "mere" information, even carefully selected information, American elementary education has become fatally one-sided. Those who have entered the teaching profession over the past forty years have been taught to scorn the mere imparting of information to children.

Thus it came about that many educators, armed with partly

true slogans, took leave of common sense. Seeing their enemy as a cruel and joyless mode of schooling, they persuaded themselves that their image of endless memorization of facts was a very real dragon that had to be slain. Even today, after forty years of domination by antifact slogans, the dragon of "rote learning" is still imagined to guard the elementary school door, despite current failures which suggest that the new dispensations are in danger of turning into dragons themselves. Hard as it is to achieve a balanced view, we owe it to our children to do so. The first step for parents and teachers who are committed to reform is to decline to be bullied by oversimplified slogans (like "learning to learn") which have not worked.

Many parents and teachers have come to the conclusion that elementary education must strike a better balance between the development of the whole child and the narrower but essential duty of the school to ensure that all children master a core of information that is necessary to their competence as learners in later grades. A great majority of parents and at least half the teachers I have spoken to have reached this conclusion through their own firsthand observations. But they cannot act on their convictions without access to an agreed-upon core sequence or concrete materials. Our main motivation in producing this series has been to give parents and teachers something concrete to work with.

Parents and teachers are urged to join in a grass-roots effort to restore balance to schooling by instituting core-knowledge standards in elementary school. The place to start is in your own school and district. You are also invited to become a member of the Core Knowledge Network by writing the Core Knowledge Foundation, 2012-B Morton Drive, Charlottesville, VA 22901.

Good luck to our children!

E. D. Hirsch, Jr.
Charlottesville, Virginia

How to Use This Book

1. Reading and Listening as an Active Adventure

A wonderful way for a child to learn is to interact with someone who is reading aloud. Active, engaged learning is remembered better than passive learning. Many adults, when reading aloud, instinctively draw children into the story by asking them questions, thus helping them to learn for themselves and to connect the narrative with their experience. All subject matters are appropriate for this interactive mode of reading aloud to children. Take for example the following passage from this volume's section on "Life Sciences":

> People have said that there are three main kinds of things in the world—animals, plants, and minerals. Animals and plants are living things, but minerals are nonliving things. Sand is a mineral. Grass is a plant. Birds and people are animals. Is it true that *everything* is animal, plant, or mineral, or some combination of these?

What rich possibilities of learning can be exploited in this very plain, short exposition! For instance, you might ask a child:

"Is it true that *everything* is animal, plant, or mineral? What about that window?"

"It's mineral."

"Okay, you're right. The *glass* is mineral, but what about the wooden frame? Is it mineral, too?"

"Yes."

"But wood comes from trees. Are trees plants, or minerals, or animals?"

"Plants."

"Right. Wood is plant; so the window is both plant and mineral."

Depending on the child's stage of development, the subject

could be taken further. A particular advantage of interactive reading is its potential to stimulate a child's curiosity and further learning by using actual objects and experiences. Such "hands-on" activities and discussions are thought to be the best way to learn about science—and other subjects, too.

The writers of this book have tried to encourage interaction with children in the stories themselves. But nothing can replace the active participation of adults as they help children enter into the vivid meaning of what is read.

2. Repetition

Do not hesitate to read sections aloud more than once. Young children like to hear good stories over and over again. The joy children take from repetition comes partly from the pleasure all people take in what is familiar and expected, but it also comes from their pleasure in fulfilling an instinct to learn securely, and truly to *possess* knowledge.

More advice to parents and teachers about teaching the specific subject matter is provided in the introduction to each section.

Joyful reading!

Introduction to Familiar Rhymes and Stories

FOR PARENTS AND TEACHERS

By first grade, many children will already recognize the traditional little rhymes presented in the following pages. Parents may wonder why they appear here in a first-grade book instead of in one for kindergarten. We decided *not* to create a book for kindergarten right away because it isn't a required year of school in every locality. We wanted to be sure that *every* first-grader who uses the book is given a chance to know who Humpty Dumpty is, and what it was that frightened Miss Muffet away.

Why did our committees include in the school core such "trivial" little verses, some of them pretty nonsensical? When Abraham Lincoln spoke of the "mystic chords of memory" that unite us, he had in mind a multiplicity of small things, some going back to the cradle, which add up to large things. We often remember best what we learned first, and among the "mystic chords of memory" few echoes are more vivid than these small fragments of rhyme from our early years.

Many of the verses are so ancient that they have no single correct version. We have chosen the versions that are most widely known in the United States. Some of the rhymes like "Three Blind Mice" and "Sing a Song of Sixpence" are traditionally sung to tunes. Others like "This Little Pig Went to Market" (a toe-counting game), involve "hands-on" activities.

A child who knows some of these rhymes by heart and who follows the words on the page as they are read aloud will gain an advantage in identifying words and letters. A child who already knows these rhymes can also gain by rereading them here with a parent or teacher who makes opportunities to build on that knowledge. "A Diller, a Dollar," for example, can be connected to learning to tell time. Discussing "Early to Bed," one might ask, what if someone gets up late, will she be healthy, wealthy, and wise? And what if they go to bed late and get up early? And many of the rhymes can be turned into counting games.

I.

LANGUAGE ARTS

There are many ways to tell the stories we have included here. You might want to supplement our versions with others you can find at the library.

Among the stories will be found three that have not been widely familiar across the land. They are "Anansi Rides Tiger," "Medio Pollito," and "Why the Owl Has Big Eyes." These are beloved stories from African-American, Hispanic, and American-Indian traditions. We hope these fine tales will become part of the American tradition.

About Stories and Poems

There are stories so magical or funny or exciting that they have delighted people for longer than anyone can remember. The word "folk" is another way to say people, so we call these stories folk tales because people told and retold them down through the ages.

Now you can find many folk tales in books, but by the time they were written down we no longer knew for sure who made them up or why. One thing is certain, though. Anytime you hear or read stories like "Cinderella" or "Little Red Riding Hood" their magic lives again.

Who Was Mother Goose?

Can you draw a picture of Mother Goose? For some people, she is a white goose wearing a floppy hat. For others, she is an old woman, seated on a rickety chair with children all around her. People in many different countries have talked about her for hundreds of years.

Whether Mother Goose was a wise old woman or a magical goose, no one knows. But the name Mother Goose has always meant good poems and stories.

People say that Mother Goose first gave us nursery rhymes, the songs and poems like "Ring Around the Rosey" that are just right for jumping rope, figuring out who goes first, or for just saying out loud. What are your favorite nursery rhymes?

FAMILIAR RHYMES

A Diller, a Dollar

A diller, a dollar,
A ten o'clock scholar,
    What makes you come so soon?
You used to come at ten o'clock
But now you come at noon!

Early to Bed

Early to bed and early to rise,
Makes a man healthy, wealthy,
        and wise.

Diddle, Diddle, Dumpling

Diddle, diddle, dumpling, my son John,
Went to bed with his stockings on;
One shoe off, and one shoe on,
Diddle, diddle, dumpling, my son John.

Jack Sprat

Jack Sprat could eat no fat,
    His wife could eat no lean,
And so between the two of them
    They licked the platter clean.

Baa, Baa, Black Sheep

Baa, baa, black sheep,
    Have you any wool?
Yes, sir, yes sir,
    Three bags full.
One for the master,
    And one for the dame,
And one for the little boy
    Who lives down the lane.

Ladybug, Ladybug

Ladybug, ladybug
    Fly away home,
Your house is on fire,
    And your children are gone.

Georgie Porgie

Georgie Porgie, pudding and pie,
Kissed the girls and made them cry;
When the boys came out to play,
Georgie Porgie ran away.

Jack and Jill

Jack and Jill went up the hill
    To fetch a pail of water;
Jack fell down and broke his crown,
    And Jill came tumbling after.

Hey, Diddle, Diddle

Hey, diddle, diddle,
The cat and the fiddle
The cow jumped over the moon;
The little dog laughed
To see such sport,
And the dish ran away with the spoon.

Hickory, Dickory, Dock

Hickory, dickory, dock,
The mouse ran up the clock.
    The clock struck one,
    The mouse ran down,
Hickory, dickory, dock.

Hot Cross Buns!

Hot cross buns!
Hot cross buns!
One a penny, two a penny,
Hot cross buns!

If you have no daughters
Give them to your sons;
One a penny, two a penny,
Hot cross buns!

Here We Go Round the Mulberry Bush

Here we go round the mulberry bush,
    The mulberry bush, the mulberry bush,
Here we go round the mulberry bush,
    So early in the morning.

Little Boy Blue

Little Boy Blue,
    Come blow your horn,
The sheep's in the meadow,
    The cow's in the corn;
But where is the boy
    Who looks after the sheep?
He's under a haystack,
    Fast asleep.

London Bridge Is Falling Down

London Bridge is falling down,
Falling down, falling down,
London Bridge is falling down,
My fair lady!

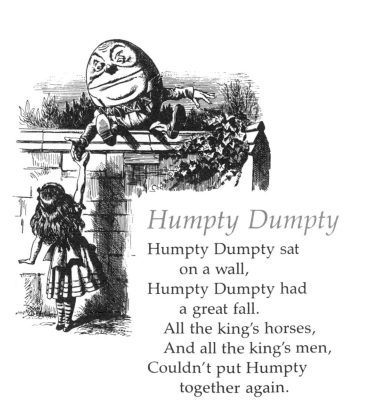

Humpty Dumpty

Humpty Dumpty sat
    on a wall,
Humpty Dumpty had
    a great fall.
All the king's horses,
    And all the king's men,
Couldn't put Humpty
    together again.

Jack Be Nimble

Jack be nimble,
Jack be quick,
Jack jump over
The candlestick.

Mary, Mary, Quite Contrary

Mary, Mary, Quite Contrary
  How does your garden grow?
With silver bells, and cockle shells,
  And pretty maids all in a row.

Mary Had a Little Lamb

Mary had a little lamb,
  Its fleece was white as snow;
And everywhere that Mary went
  The lamb was sure to go.

It followed her to school one day,
  That was against the rule;
It made the children laugh and play
  To see a lamb at school.

And so the teacher turned it out,
  But still it lingered near;
And waited patiently about
  Till Mary did appear.

"Why does the lamb love Mary so?"
  The eager children cry.
"Why Mary loves the lamb, you know,"
  The teacher did reply.

Little Miss Muffet

Little Miss Muffet
Sat on a tuffet,
Eating her curds and whey;
Along came a spider,
Who sat down beside her
And frightened Miss Muffet away.

Old King Cole

Old King Cole
Was a merry old soul
And a merry old soul was he;
He called for his pipe,
And he called for his bowl,
And he called for his fiddlers three.

Little Jack Horner

Little Jack Horner
Sat in a corner,
Eating his Christmas pie;
He put in his thumb,
And pulled out a plum,
And said, "What a good boy am I!"

Little Bo Peep

Little Bo Peep has lost her sheep,
 And can't tell where to find them;
Leave them alone, and they'll come home,
 Wagging their tails behind them.

One, Two, Buckle My Shoe

One, two,
Buckle my shoe;
Three, four,
Shut the door;
Five, six,
Pick up sticks;
Seven, eight,
Lay them straight;
Nine, ten,
A big fat hen;
Eleven, twelve,
Dig and delve;
Thirteen, fourteen,
Maids a-courting;
Fifteen, sixteen,
Maids in the kitchen;
Seventeen, eighteen,
Maids in waiting;
Nineteen, twenty,
My plate's empty.

Pat-a-Cake

Pat-a-cake, pat-a-cake, baker's man!
Bake me a cake as fast as you can.
Pat it and prick it and mark it with a "B,"
And put it in the oven for baby and me.

Ring Around the Rosey

Ring around the rosey,
A pocket full of posies.
Ashes, ashes,
We all fall down.

The Owl and the Pussycat by Edward Lear

I

The owl and the pussycat went to sea
    In a beautiful pea-green boat,
They took some honey, and plenty of money,
    Wrapped up in a five-pound note.
The owl looked up to the stars above,
    And sang to a small guitar,
"O lovely Pussy! O Pussy, my love,
    What a beautiful Pussy you are,
        You are,
        You are!
What a beautiful Pussy you are!"

II

Pussy said to the owl, "You elegant fowl!
    How charmingly sweet you sing!
O let us be married! Too long have we tarried:
    But what shall we do for a ring?"
They sailed away for a year and a day,
    To the land where the bong-tree grows
And there in a wood a piggy-wig stood
    With a ring at the end of his nose,
        His nose,
        His nose,
    With a ring at the end of his nose.

"Dear Pig, are you willing to sell for one shilling
    Your ring?" Said the piggy, "I will."
So they took it away, and were married next day
    By the turkey who lives on the hill.
They dined on mince, and slices of quince,
    Which they ate with a runcible spoon;
And hand in hand, on the edge of the sand,
    They danced by the light of the moon,
        The moon,
        The moon,
They danced by the light of the moon.

Tom, Tom, the Piper's Son

Tom, Tom, the piper's son,
Stole a pig, and away he run.
The pig was eat, and Tom was beat,
And Tom went crying down the street.

See-Saw, Margery Daw

See-Saw, Margery Daw
Jack shall have a new master;
Jack must have but a penny a day,
Because he can't work any faster.

Old Mother Hubbard

Old Mother Hubbard,
Went to the cupboard,
    To get her poor dog a bone,
But when she got there,
The cupboard was bare,
    And so her poor dog had none.

Star Light, Star Bright

Star light, star bright,
First star I see tonight,
I wish I may, I wish I might,
Have the wish I wish tonight.

Rock-a-bye, Baby

Rock-a-bye, baby
In the tree top,
When the wind blows,
The cradle will rock.

When the bough breaks,
The cradle will fall,
And down will come baby,
Cradle and all.

Ride a Cock-horse

Ride a cock-horse to Banbury Cross,
To see a fine lady upon a white horse;
With rings on her fingers and bells on her toes,
She shall have music wherever she goes.

Sing a Song of Sixpence

Sing a song of sixpence,
    A pocket full of rye;
Four and twenty blackbirds
    Baked in a pie.

When the pie was opened,
    The birds began to sing;
Wasn't that a dainty dish
    To set before the king?

The king was in his counting-house
    Counting out his money;
The queen was in the parlor
    Eating bread and honey.

The maid was in the garden
    Hanging out the clothes,
Along came a blackbird
    And nipped off her nose.

Rub-a-dub-dub

Rub-a-dub-dub,
Three men in a tub;
And who do you think they be?
The butcher, the baker,
The candlestick maker;
Turn them out, knaves all three!

Rain, Rain, Go Away

Rain, rain, go away,
Come again another day.

Roses Are Red

Roses are red,
    Violets are blue,
Sugar is sweet,
    And so are you.

There Was a Little Girl

There was a little girl, and she had a little curl
   Right in the middle of her forehead;
When she was good, she was very, very good,
   But when she was bad, she was horrid.

Twinkle, Twinkle, Little Star

Twinkle, twinkle, little star,
How I wonder what you are.
Up above the world so high
Like a diamond in the sky.
Twinkle, twinkle, little star,
How I wonder what you are!

Three Blind Mice

Three blind mice,
Three blind mice,
See how they run!
See how they run!
They all ran after the farmer's wife,
Who cut off their tails with a carving knife,
Did you ever see such a sight in your life,
   As three blind mice?

Simple Simon

Simple Simon met a pieman
   Going to the fair;
Said Simple Simon to the pieman,
   "Let me taste your ware."

Says the pieman to Simple Simon,
   "Show me first your penny";
Says Simple Simon to the pieman,
   "Indeed, I have not any."

There Was an Old Woman Who Lived in a Shoe

There was an old woman who lived in a shoe,
She had so many children she didn't know what to do;
She gave them some broth without any bread;
And spanked them all soundly and put them to bed.

This Little Pig Went to Market

This little piggy went to market,
This little piggy stayed home,
This little piggy had roast beef,
And this little piggy had none,
And this little piggy cried, Wee-wee-wee-wee,
All the way home.

STORIES

Anansi Rides Tiger

Linda was the most beautiful girl in town, and Anansi the Spider and Brer Tiger were both in love with her. Brer Tiger figured he had nothing to worry about. With eyes that shone like emeralds and his slick fur coat, he was the most powerful cat around. And Anansi? He was just a puny spider.

But one day, Linda didn't greet Brer Tiger in her usual way. "How can I marry you?" she said. "Anansi says you're just his old riding horse!"

"Riding horse?" Brer Tiger roared with outrage. "I'm not his riding horse."

Linda didn't know what to think. All of the animals were talking about it. Anansi said he rode Tiger just like a horse. "Prove it," she said.

Brer Tiger thundered off, and all of the animals in the jungle ran for cover. When he reached Anansi's house, he nearly crushed the front door with his pounding. "Come out here, you little liar!"

A thin, tired voice answered, "This is Anansi. Tiger, I have a fever, and I'm too weak to move. I'm near to dying."

Tiger bounded into the house. "You can't die before you tell Linda the truth. She thinks I'm your riding horse."

Anansi laughed weakly. "I never said that Tiger. Please, let me die in peace."

Tiger wouldn't hear of it. "You can't die before you tell her. If you're so weak, you old spider, I'll carry you there."

Anansi said tiredly, "Oh, all right. But I'll need a fly swatter so that those jungle flies don't eat me alive. And I'm so weak, I'll need a rope to tie around your neck that I can hang on to. And a blanket," Anansi said. "For my sore old body."

Tiger growled, but agreed.

And so it was that Linda and her friends looked up from her front porch to see Tiger striding toward them with Anansi, riding straight as an arrow, on his back. When Linda's eyes widened with surprise, Anansi dug his heels into his blanket saddle, pulled his rope reins, and slapped Tiger with his swatter. He shouted, "See, Linda, what did I tell you. Giddyup, Tiger!"

Poor Tiger bucked and bucked until Anansi let go of him, and then Tiger ran into the jungle never to see Linda again.

Chicken Little

One day as Chicken Little was walking in the woods an acorn fell on her head. "The sky is falling!" she said. "I must go and tell the King."

So she want along until she met Henny Penny. "Henny Penny, the sky is falling!" said Chicken Little.

"How do you know?" said Henny Penny.

"A piece of it fell upon my head," said Chicken Little.

"Then let us go and tell the King!" said Henny Penny.

So Henny Penny and Chicken Little went along until they met Goosey Poosey.

"Goosey Poosey, the sky is falling!" said Henny Penny.

"How do you know?" said Goosey Poosey.

"A piece of it fell upon my head," said Chicken Little.

"Then let us go and tell the King!" said Goosey Poosey.

So Goosey Poosey, Henny Penny, and Chicken Little went along until they met Cocky Locky.

"Cocky Locky, the sky is falling!" said Goosey Poosey.

"How do you know?" said Cocky Locky.

"A piece of it fell upon my head," said Chicken Little.

"Then let us go and tell the King!" said Cocky Locky.

So Cocky Locky, Goosey Poosey, Henny Penny, and Chicken Little went along until they met Turkey Lurkey.

"Turkey Lurkey, the sky is falling!" said Cocky Locky.

"How do you know?" said Turkey Lurkey.

"A piece of it fell upon my head," said Chicken Little.

"Then let us go and tell the King!" said Turkey Lurkey. So they went along until they met Foxy Woxy.

"Foxy Woxy, the sky is falling!" said Turkey Lurkey.

"Oh, is that so?" said sly Foxy Woxy.

"If the sky is falling, you'd better keep safe at my den, and I will tell the King."

So Chicken Little, Henny Penny, Goosey Poosey, Cocky Locky, and Turkey Lurkey followed Foxy Woxy into his den, where he ate them up, every one.

Cinderella

Once upon a time there was a kind and beautiful girl who was left with no one in the world except a cruel stepmother and two selfish stepsisters. While the stepsisters spent their days primping before the mirror, she was given only rags to wear and forced to clean the house and wait on them. This she did cheerfully, keeping her troubles to herself. At night the poor girl had to sleep upon the hearth among the cinders. For this reason they called her "Cinderella."

One day the prince invited all the young ladies in the kingdom to a grand ball at the palace. The stepsisters could talk of nothing but fancy dresses and dancing with the prince. They kept Cinderella busy for days preparing their gowns, shoes, and hair, and as she worked they made fun of her. "You can't go to the ball in a dress covered with ashes!" they said. Cinderella helped her sisters as well as she could and tried to ignore their teasing.

On the night of the ball, the stepmother and stepsisters rode away in their coach. Poor Cinderella sat down in the cinders and cried. Suddenly she heard a gentle voice say, "Don't weep, my dear. You, too, shall go to the ball."

Cinderella looked up and saw an old woman with a kind face.

"But how can that be?" she asked.

"You will see, dear child," said the old woman, "for I am your fairy godmother." She waved a wand and instantly transformed a pumpkin from the garden into an elegant coach. Six mice caught in a trap became six horses. Cinderella's rags were magically changed into a gown of gold and silver and on her feet appeared lovely little glass slippers. She joyfully thanked her fairy godmother.

"Now hurry," said the old woman, "but be sure to leave the ball before the clock strikes twelve, for at that moment the magic will cease!"

When Cinderella arrived at the ball, everyone turned to look at her. Who was this beautiful girl? Not even her own stepsisters recognized her. The prince bowed to her and asked, "May I have this dance?" Cinderella smiled and answered, "I would be delighted." The two danced together all evening. As they waltzed dreamily, Cinderella nearly forgot the warning. Suddenly the striking clock brought her to her senses. It was almost midnight! Without a word, she ran from the palace, climbed in her coach, and drove away. No sooner was she home again than her coach became a pumpkin, her horses became mice, and her gown became rags once more.

The prince didn't even know her name! As he ran after her, he found one of her glass slippers lying on the ground. "I must marry the girl who can wear this slipper," he declared.

The next day he and his men searched for the shoe's owner, coming at long last to Cinderella's house. The excited stepsisters came forward, and each one struggled to cram her large foot into the dainty shoe. They would have given their toes to marry the prince! But at last they gave up trying.

"Please," asked the prince, "is there no other young lady here? We have tried all the houses in the kingdom." Cinderella stepped from the dark corner and asked, "May I try?" "You!" mocked the stepmother. "Go back to the cinders where you belong!" But the prince insisted that she try on the slipper. It fit perfectly. He fell upon his knees and asked Cinderella to be his wife, and her stepmother and stepsisters begged her forgiveness.

Cinderella washed the cinders from her face, put on a royal gown, and married the prince in fine style. Kind as always, Cinderella invited her stepmother and sisters to live at the palace, and Cinderella and the prince lived in great happiness.

Goldilocks and the Three Bears

Once upon a time a curious little girl named Goldilocks lived with her mother at the edge of a deep forest. One day as she was playing, she began to wander into the woods. Soon she could no longer see her house, but still she walked on. At last she came to a cute little cottage among the trees. When she saw that the door was open, she walked right in.

On the table she saw three steaming bowls of porridge, a big bowl, a middle-sized bowl, and a little tiny bowl. She began to feel very hungry. She tasted the porridge in the biggest bowl, but found it too hot. The porridge in the middle-sized bowl was too cold.

But the porridge in the little tiny bowl was just right, so she ate every drop. Then she saw three chairs in the room and decided to sit down and relax. The big chair was too hard and the middle-sized chair was too soft. But the little chair was just right, so she plopped down with a happy sigh—and the chair collapsed! She looked for another place to rest. Upstairs she found three beds. The big one was much too hard, and the middle-sized one was a bit too soft. But the cozy little bed was just right, so Goldilocks snuggled down and was soon asleep.

What Goldilocks didn't know was that she was in the house of three bears—a mother bear, a father bear, and a baby bear. Each morning these three bears left their cottage to take a walk while their breakfast porridge cooled. No sooner had Goldilocks fallen asleep than the bears returned, hungry for their breakfast. When Papa Bear saw the big bowl, he roared loudly, "Someone's been eating my porridge!"

Then Mama Bear looked at the middle-sized bowl. In a low, angry voice she said, "And someone's been eating my porridge!" Then Baby Bear saw the little, tiny bowl and began to cry in a high, squeaky voice, "And

someone's been eating *my* porridge and has eaten it all up!" Then Papa Bear saw his chair. "Someone's been sitting in my chair!" he bellowed loudly. "And someone's been sitting in *my* chair!" grumbled Mama as she fluffed up the seat cushion. "And someone's been sitting in *my* chair and has broken it all to pieces!" hollered Baby Bear, bursting into tears.

The three bears marched upstairs. Papa and Mama spotted the rumpled bedspreads. "Someone's been sleeping in my bed!" he said. "And someone's been sleeping in my bed," she echoed. "And someone's been sleeping in *my* bed and is still there!" yelled Baby Bear. The shouting woke up Goldilocks, who turned pale at the sight of the three bears. She leaped out of bed and ran down the stairs and out the cottage door, and she didn't stop until she was safe in her mother's arms.

Would you like to act out this story? Get three of your friends to help you. One of you can be Goldilocks, one can be Baby Bear, one Papa Bear, and one Mama Bear.

Jack and the Beanstalk

Once upon a time there was a poor widow who was barely able to afford enough food to feed herself and her son, whose name was Jack. One day she said, "Jack, we have nothing left in the cupboard. You must take the cow to town and sell her so that we can have money for food." Jack did as he was told and set off for town, leading the cow behind him. Very soon he came back all alone. "See what I got for our cow, Mother," he said proudly. "I sold her to a man for three magic beans."

When Jack's mother heard that he had traded their cow for three beans, she was furious. "Foolish boy!" she cried. "Three beans cannot keep us from starving!" She threw the beans out of the window and sent Jack to bed.

The next morning Jack and his mother were surprised to see that a gigantic vine had sprung from the very spot where the beans had landed. It rose above the house and disappeared into the clouds high overhead. Jack began to climb the vine and soon he had disappeared into the clouds, too.

At the top of the vine Jack found a huge, magnificent castle with a door ten times his size. He knocked as hard as he could and called out, "Please, have you any food to spare for a hungry boy?" The door swung open, and Jack looked with fright upon a woman who was as tall as a tree. She lifted him up by his shirt and placed him on a table. "You're hungry, are you?" she said. "Well, I'll give you a bite to eat. But watch out for my husband! He would like nothing better than to take a bite of *you!*" And with that, she handed Jack a slice of bread as big as a mattress, and a piece of cheese high enough to sit upon.

But before Jack could eat, he heard giant-sized footsteps. A giant-sized voice said gruffly, "Wife, where's my dinner?" Jack hid out of sight in the shadows. Then he heard the giant man say,

"Fee, fie, fo, fum
I smell the blood of an Eng-lish-man
Be he alive, or be he dead,
I'll grind his bones to make my bread!"

"Nonsense, dear," said his wife. "Now sit down and have some bread and cheese." The giant ate the bread and cheese that had been meant for Jack, and then had three whole chickens and a gallon of milk as well. When he was full, he stretched in his chair and yawned. "Wife," he said rudely, "bring my hen and my harp!" She opened a cage and gently lifted out a snow white hen, which she placed before the giant. "Hen, lay!" he demanded. The hen laid a solid gold egg. Then the wife lifted a beautiful golden harp from a nail on the wall and placed it before the giant. "Harp, play!" he ordered. All by itself, the harp began to play a pretty lullaby. Soon the giant was sound asleep.

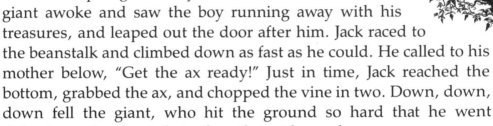

Jack saw that this was his chance to escape, but he could not bear to leave the hen and harp with the mean giant. "How pleased my mother would be if I brought them to her!" he said to himself. He dashed from the shadows, tucked the hen under his arm, slung the harp over his back, and hopped nimbly to the floor. He ran out of the door and would have escaped easily, but the harp began to cry, "Thief! Thief!" The giant awoke and saw the boy running away with his treasures, and leaped out the door after him. Jack raced to the beanstalk and climbed down as fast as he could. He called to his mother below, "Get the ax ready!" Just in time, Jack reached the bottom, grabbed the ax, and chopped the vine in two. Down, down, down fell the giant, who hit the ground so hard that he went right through the earth to the other side, and was never seen again. Afterward, Jack and his mother never lacked money or music, for the hen gave them golden eggs, and the harp played for them all day long.

The Little Red Hen

Once a hard-working little red hen lived with a dog, cat, and pig. One day she decided to make bread. "Who will help me cut the wheat to make my bread?" she asked. "Not I," said the dog sleepily. "Not I," yawned the cat. "Not I," grunted the pig.

"Then I will do it myself," she said. When she had cut the wheat, the little red hen asked, "Who will help me take the wheat to the miller for grinding?" "Not I," growled the dog. "Not I," hissed the cat. "Not I," snorted the pig. "Then I will do it myself," said the little red hen.

When the wheat had been ground into flour, the little red hen asked, "Who will help me make the flour into bread dough?" "Not I," sighed the dog. "Not I," whined the cat. "Not I," sniffed the pig. "Then I will do it myself," she said. When she had mixed the dough, the little red hen asked, "Who will help me bake the bread?" "Not I," muttered the dog. "Not I," murmured the cat. "Not I," grumbled the pig. "Then I will do it myself," she said.

Soon the wonderful smell of freshly baked bread filled the kitchen. "Now," said the little red hen, "who will help me eat the bread?" "I will!" barked the dog, his tail wagging. "I will," purred the cat. "I will!" grunted the pig happily. But the little red hen said, "Not so fast! I cut the wheat all by myself. I took it to the mill and brought home the flour, all by myself. I mixed the dough and baked it, all by myself. And now I shall eat the bread, all by myself!" So as the little red hen tasted the delicious warm bread, the unhappy dog, cat, and pig sat beside her and hungrily watched every bite.

Little Red Riding Hood

There was once a little girl who was called Little Red Riding Hood because she always wore a red cloak with a hood. One morning her mother said, "Little Red Riding Hood, your grandma isn't feeling well. I want you to take her this cider and cake." Red Riding Hood loved her grandma very much and was eager to do as her mother asked. "Now don't stray from the path," her mother cautioned, "and don't speak to strangers!" The child promised to obey as she took the basket and skipped off.

The path to Grandma's house led through a forest where there lurked a hungry wolf. As Red Riding Hood skipped along, he suddenly stepped out in front of her. Since she knew nothing about wolves, she wasn't at all frightened and politely asked him to let her pass. "Of course I'll let you pass," he said, "but tell me, where are you going and what is in your basket?" "I'm taking goodies to Grandma, who is sick," she said. "And where does Grandma live?" he asked. "In the cottage between the chestnut trees," she answered without thinking that it was really none of his business. "Is that so?" said the sly wolf. "Well, why not stop to pick some flowers for her? Think how pleased she'll be!" What a good idea, thought Red Riding Hood. She thanked the wolf and wandered from the path to a field of wildflowers, where she spent quite a time selecting just the right ones for Grandma's bouquet.

Meanwhile the hungry wolf slipped away and reached Grandma's cottage first. He knocked, and the grandmother called in a feeble voice, "Who's there?"

The wolf tried to sound like a little girl. "It is I, Red Riding Hood."

"Just lift the latch and come in," said Grandma. So the wolf rushed in and gobbled her up in one bite. Then he dressed himself in a nightgown and nightcap and hid under the covers to wait for Red Riding Hood.

In a little while he heard her knock. Now he changed his voice to sound like a grandmother. "Just lift the latch and come in," he called.

Red Riding Hood tiptoed toward the bed with a worried look. "Why, Grandma, what big eyes you have!"

"The better to see you with, my dear," said the furry-faced Grandma.

"But, Grandma, what big ears you have!"

"The better to hear you with, my dear."

"And, Grandma, what big teeth you have!"

"The better to EAT you with!" growled the wolf, and he threw off the covers, pounced upon Red Riding Hood, and swallowed her in one gulp. Then, with a very full tummy, he fell sound asleep in the grandmother's bed.

A woodcutter who often stopped to chat with Grandma happened by, and was alarmed to hear the wolf's loud snoring. "I'd better see what's wrong," he said. He pushed open the door and was horrified to see the fat, sleeping wolf. The woodcutter raised his ax and cut open the wolf's stomach. Out popped Little Red Riding Hood and her grandmother, alive and well! They quickly gathered enough large stones to fill the sleeping wolf's belly, then sewed him up again and hid out of sight. The wolf awoke with a bad tummy ache and wandered off into the woods, and he never had an appetite for grandmas or little girls again.

Medio Pollito

There was once a large black Spanish hen who had fine little chicks. All of them were ordinary chicks, except for one, who looked as if he had been cut right in half. All his brothers and sisters had two wings and two legs, and two eyes, but he had only one of each. And he had only half a head and half a beak. So they called him Medio Pollito, which means "Half-Chick" in Spanish.

The brother and sister chicks did just what they were told to do, but Medio Pollito did not like to obey his mother. When mother hen called for him to come back to the chicken house, he pretended that he could not hear, because he had only one ear. And the older he became, the more he disobeyed his mother.

One day he said: "I am tired of life in the barnyard. I am going to the city to see the King."

His mother said, "You aren't old enough yet. When you get older, we will go to the city together."

But Medio Pollito would not listen to anyone. "I am going to visit the King, and I shall have a big house in the city, and become rich, and maybe I will invite you to visit me sometime." With that, he hopped down the road toward the city. His mother called out: "Be sure to be nice to everyone you meet." But Medio did not listen, and off he went.

He first hopped to a little stream of water, choked with weeds. "Oh, Medio," it cried, "please help me clear away these weeds, so I can flow."

"Do you think I have time to take from my travels?" said Medio. "I am off to the city to see the King." And away he hopped.

Later he came to some burning grass, and the fire said to him, "Medio, please put some sticks on me, so I won't go out."

"Do you think I have time to take from my travels?" said Medio. "I am off to the city to see the King." And away he hopped.

As he got closer to the city he came to a tree where the wind was caught in the branches and leaves, and the wind said to Medio: "Oh, please climb up here and get me out of these branches, so I can fly away."

"Do you think I have time to take from my travels?" said Medio. "I am off to the city to see the King." And away he hopped.

As he entered the city, he saw the royal palace, and hopped right into the courtyard. Who should see Medio but the King's cook, who said: "I think I shall make the King a nice chicken soup for dinner." And he reached out, and caught Medio, and put him into a pot of water near the stove.

Medio felt very wet. "Oh, water," he cried, "don't wet me like this." But the water replied: "You would not help me when I was a little stream, so why should I help you?"

Then the fire on the stove began to heat the water. Medio felt very hot. "Oh, fire," he cried, "don't burn me like this." But the fire replied, "You would not help me when I was going out in the grass, so why should I help you?"

The pain was so bad that Medio thought he would die. Just then, the cook raised the lid of the pot to see if the soup was ready. But he saw the ugly little chick, and said: "I can't send such an ugly chick to the King." And he threw Medio out the window.

There the wind caught him and took him so fast he could hardly breathe. "Oh, wind," he cried, "don't carry me like this. Let me rest or I shall die." But

the wind replied: "You would not help me when I was caught in the tree, so why should I help you?" And with that he lifted up Medio Pollito, up in the air to the top of the church tower, and left him stuck on the steeple.

There he is to this very day. If you look at the top of many a church steeple, you will see a weather vane in the form of half a chicken. It is Medio Pollito, the chick who would not help others. Now he must help everyone by showing them which way the wind is blowing.

Peter Rabbit

Once there was a mother rabbit who lived in a hole in the sand bank with her four children, Flopsy, Mopsy, Cottontail, and Peter. One morning Mrs. Rabbit said to the children, "I want you to go out and pick some blackberries for supper. Have a good time, but whatever you do, stay out of Mr. McGregor's garden! Your father had an accident there and was baked into

a pie by Mrs. McGregor." Now Flopsy, Mopsy, and Cottontail were good little bunnies, but Peter was always getting into mischief. Instead of picking blackberries, he ran straight to Mr. McGregor's garden and squeezed under the gate.

Peter ran about tasting lettuces, radishes, and other delights. Then, feeling a little sick, he looked around for some parsley to nibble. Suddenly, who should appear but Mr. McGregor! He chased Peter all around the garden, while the frightened little bunny looked everywhere for the gate. First Peter lost both his shoes, and then he snagged his coat on a gooseberry net. He wriggled out of his coat just in time to escape Mr. McGregor's sieve, which was coming down to trap him.

At last Peter ducked into the toolshed, where he hid in a big watering can. It was half-filled with water, and Peter was very uncomfortable as he waited for Mr. McGregor to go away. Finally Mr. McGregor grew tired of looking for Peter and went back to his work. He used Peter's shoes and coat to make a scarecrow to keep the birds out of the garden.

Peter hopped out of the toolshed window and onto a wheelbarrow. From here he could see Mr. McGregor and the garden gate just beyond him! He ran as fast as he could right past Mr. McGregor and squeezed under the gate just in time. Peter didn't stop running until he was lying safe on the soft sand of his rabbit hole. His mother wondered where his clothes had gone. This was the second coat he had lost in two weeks!

Peter was not feeling very well that evening, so his mother sent him straight to bed and gave him a dose of chamomile tea. But Flopsy, Mopsy, and Cottontail had blackberries and cream for dinner.

The Pied Piper of Hamelin

In the town of Hamelin, there once lived a great many rats. There were rats in all the houses, rats in the shops, rats in the churches, and rats in the school. Though the townfolk tried and tried to get rid of them, the rats only became more plentiful. They soon began to take over the town, going where they pleased in broad daylight, stealing food right off dinner plates, and even curling up to sleep on people's beds.

The people of Hamelin held a town meeting to decide how to get rid of the rats. "I have an idea," said the mayor. "Let us offer a reward to anyone who can solve our problem." "Yes, yes," all the people agreed. "Let the reward be a sack of gold coins!" And so they sent word far and wide that a sack of gold coins would be given to anyone who could rid Hamelin of its rats.

Not long afterward, a stranger appeared in town. He was dressed in all the colors of the rainbow, and he seemed to dance when he walked. The people on the street wondered who he might be, so they followed him until he arrived at the mayor's door. "I have come to rid your town of rats," he said to the mayor. The mayor laughed at him. "What a silly-looking fellow you are," he said. "How can you possibly rid our town of rats?" "You will see," said the man. "And if I do, you must give me a sack of gold coins, for that is

the reward you have named." "Why, of course," said the mayor. "A sack of gold is the least we can give for such a service. Now, show us what you can do."

The stranger took from his belt a little set of shepherd's pipes, put them to his lips, and began to play a tune. Immediately, the rats on the street pricked up their ears and hurried toward the sound. The stranger began walking toward the edge of town, piping his tune all the while. From every shop, house, and shed all over the town, the rats poured until the streets were filled with them. They followed the piper out of the town and down the road to the edge of the river. Then the rats jumped in and were carried far away by the rushing water.

There was not a single rat left in Hamelin. The people of the town held a day-long celebration. "What a clever fellow that piper is!" they all said. The piper went to the mayor once more. "Now I would like the sack of gold you promised me," he said.

The mayor frowned and said, "A sack of gold is a great reward for so easy a task. All you did was play a tune!" When the people of the town heard the mayor, they began to think that the piper was not so clever after all. "Yes, that's true," they said. "He only played a tune. Why should we pay him?"

"You will pay for my piping one way or another," said the stranger. He put his pipe to his lips once more and began to play a different tune—a tune that made everyone feel strangely nervous. Suddenly, from every open doorway, every sunny courtyard, and every fragrant garden, the children of Hamelin came running to follow the piper. The parents cried out in fear as they guessed what was happening, but they could do nothing to stop it. Laughing and skipping, the children followed the dancing piper down the street to the edge of town and on toward the faraway mountains. There, the door to fairyland opened and took them in. Then it closed behind them forever.

Pinocchio

Once a poor woodcarver named Geppetto found a piece of wood that could talk. He carved it into a puppet which he named Pinocchio. Pinocchio was full of life and he often got into trouble. One day he even burned his feet in the fire, and Geppetto had to make him new ones. A talking cricket warned Pinocchio that he must learn to be good.

Geppetto sold his only jacket to buy an ABC book for his son. Pinocchio set off for school, and I'm sure he would have gone there if he hadn't happened upon a puppet show. Before he knew it, he had traded his new book for a ticket. He danced with the puppets in the show until the mean puppet master appeared. He wanted to throw a puppet on the fire! Pinocchio bravely said, "Please spare this puppet. You can burn me instead—though it will grieve my poor old papa." His words made the puppet master feel sorry. He promised to spare all the puppets. Then he gave Pinocchio five gold coins to take home.

Pinocchio was taking them to his papa, when he met a fox and a cat. "If you will bury your money in a certain field," said the fox, "you will soon have a tree covered with gold coins!" Pinocchio thanked him and set off alone to find the magic field. On the way he was attacked by two masked robbers. Pinocchio held his coins under his tongue, and bit off a robber's hand when he tried to take them. Why, it was not a hand, but a paw! The robbers hung Pinocchio from a tree and ran away.

A blue fairy rescued Pinocchio, and he told her the whole story. But when she asked him about the coins, he lied and said that he had lost them. All at once his nose began to grow longer and longer. "You see, Pinocchio," scolded the fairy, "a lie can grow until it's as plain as the nose on your face!" He promised never to lie again, so the fairy made his nose short once more. "Be good," she warned, "and stay away from anyone who promises you something for nothing."

If only Pinocchio had listened! On his way home, he ran into the fox and the cat, who was now missing one paw. They took him to the magic field to bury his money, then told him to go away while the tree grew. But when Pinocchio returned, there was no tree, and the coins he had buried were gone. Who could have taken them?

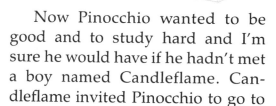

Now Pinocchio wanted to be good and to study hard and I'm sure he would have if he hadn't met a boy named Candleflame. Candleflame invited Pinocchio to go to Funland, where little boys play all day and eat candy. Off they went in a coach with lots of other boys. In Funland they did exactly as they pleased, until one day they began to turn into donkeys!

Pinocchio escaped by jumping into the sea, and was swallowed by a giant shark. Who should be in the shark's stomach but his dear papa! You see, Geppetto had been looking for Pinocchio everywhere when his boat was swallowed by the monstrous fish. Pinocchio managed to pull Geppetto up through the shark's mouth, out into the sea, and safely to land. Then Pinocchio fainted.

Suddenly the blue fairy appeared. "Pinocchio," she said, "because you have been unselfish, you may have your heart's desire." The puppet began to tingle. He looked at his hands and feet and felt his nose. His body was soft and warm. "Papa!" he cried. "I'm a real boy!" His papa threw his arms around him and they danced for joy, for their greatest wish had come true.

The Princess and the Pea

There was once a prince who wished to marry a real princess. He met many young ladies who claimed to be princesses, but he could never be sure if they really were. Besides, not one of them was right for him.

One night there was a terrible storm. The wind whistled about the turrets of the castle, and the rain pounded hard upon the roof. In the midst of all the thunder and lightning, there was a knock upon the door. The prince opened it to see a lovely girl who was dripping wet and cold. She told the prince and his mother and father that she was a princess who had lost her way. Could she stay there for the night?

Seeing that her son and the girl liked one another, the Queen said to herself, "I will find out if she is really a princess or not." She slipped into the guest bedroom and removed the mattress from the bed. Then she placed one

tiny pea upon the bedstead. On top of that she piled twenty mattresses, and on top of the mattresses, she piled twenty featherbeds! Then she sent for the girl, and told her that this huge bed was where she would spend the night.

In the morning, the Queen asked, "How did you sleep?" "Most dreadfully!" said the girl. "I hardly closed my eyes all night, for it felt as if there were something very hard beneath me, and this morning I have purple bruises all over!" Then the Queen knew that her son's bride was found, for no one but a princess could have such delicate skin. The prince and the princess were married, and the pea was put in a museum where it can still be seen. Now this is a true story.

Puss-in-Boots

Once upon a time a miller died leaving his three sons all that he owned. To his oldest son, he left his mill, and to the middle son he left his mule. But to his youngest son he left only his cat.

Seeing how downhearted his master was at his poor fortune, the cat said cheerfully, "Give me a cloth sack and a pair of boots, and I shall make things better for you." The miller's son thought this request was strange, but since he had nothing to lose but his boots, he did as the cat said.

The cat immediately went to work and caught half a dozen partridges, which he put into the sack. Then, having put his master's boots on his own feet, he carried the partridges to the King. "May it please Your Majesty," said the cat, "I have here a gift of partridges from my master, the Marquis of Carabas. He sends the King his most excellent regards." The King was very pleased, and sent his thanks in return.

The next day the King happened to be riding by as the miller's son was bathing in the river. When the cat saw the King's coach, he cried, "Help! Help!

Someone please help my master, the Marquis of Carabas! Thieves have robbed him of his clothes and thrown him in the water!" The King, remembering the gift of partridges, ordered his men to stop and help the cat's master. They pulled him out of the river and gave him a fine suit of clothes to wear. The King then invited him to ride along in the coach.

Meanwhile, the cat ran ahead until he came to some people mowing a large field with scythes. He spoke to them as if he were a very important person. "If anyone wishes to know who owns this field, you must tell them it belongs to the Marquis of Carabas," said the cat. "Else you'll be chopped up like herbs for the soup!" Then the cat ran on until he came upon some people threshing wheat in an even larger field. Again he commanded them to tell everyone that the field belonged to the Marquis of Carabas. "Else you'll be chopped up like herbs for the soup!" he said. The cat ran on until he came to a grand castle, where the real owner of the fields lived. He was an ogre who had the power to change himself into anything under the sun. The cat greeted him and said, "Oh, most powerful ogre, I have heard of your talents and have traveled far to see them for myself. Is it true that you can turn yourself into something big and fierce?" The ogre was flattered, and without hesitation he turned himself into a lion, which gave the cat quite a scare for the moment. But he quickly got hold of himself and said, "That is indeed impressive, but can you also turn yourself into something small and meek? Oh, surely you cannot do that, can you?" "Just watch me," bragged the ogre. And with that, he turned himself into a mouse, and was immediately captured and eaten by the cat.

Meanwhile, the King's coach was traveling through the ogre's lands. "Who owns these fine-looking fields?" the King asked. The mowers quickly answered,

"The Marquis of Carabas!" And again, when the King asked the threshers, "Who owns these fields?" they all replied, "the Marquis of Carabas!" At last the coach came to the ogre's castle. Out ran the cat to greet them. "Welcome home, master!" he said, "all is prepared for you." They went inside and found a magnificent feast awaiting them. You see, the ogre had been entertaining house guests, who had all run away at the sight of the King's coach.

The King was so pleased with the wealth and good taste of the Marquis of Carabas that he introduced him to his daughter. The two fell in love and decided to marry, and from that day on, the poor miller's son and his clever cat were poor no more.

Rapunzel

Once upon a time, a husband and wife were expecting a baby. One day as the wife sat looking out of her window, she saw some rapunzel lettuce growing in the garden next door. Suddenly she felt that she must have a taste of it or die, so she sent her husband to get some. He sneaked into the garden and stole a bit for her, but the taste only made her long for more. A second time, the husband sneaked into the garden, but this time he was caught by the old witch who owned it. "You'll be sorry you stole my rapunzel!" she cried. He begged her to forgive him. "Only on one condition," she said. "When your child is born, you must give it to me!" The man was afraid of the old woman's power, so he agreed. When a baby girl was born to them, the witch appeared immediately and snatched her away. She named the baby Rapunzel.

Rapunzel was a sweet, beautiful girl. The witch locked her away from the world in a high tower in the forest. All day Rapunzel sat by the window and sang to keep up her spirits. Whenever the witch wished to come up, she would stand at the foot of the tower and call, "Rapunzel, Rapunzel, let down your hair." Then Rapunzel would let her long braid fall to the ground and the witch would climb it like a rope.

One day a prince was riding through the forest, when he heard Rapunzel singing. He followed the sound until he came to the tower. How he longed to meet the girl who sang so sweetly! But he could see no way to climb the tower.

The next day he returned to the forest to hear her sing again. As he drew near, he overheard the witch say, "Rapunzel, Rapunzel, let down your hair!" He hid in the trees and watched as the old woman climbed to the window. Then, when the witch had departed once more, he himself went to the foot of the tower and called, "Rapunzel, Rapunzel, let down your hair!" The braid fell, and he climbed it to the window to look for the first time upon Rapunzel's sweet face. Naturally, she was amazed to see a beautiful young man standing before her. Soon the two found themselves falling in love. They decided that whenever the prince came to visit, he would bring a skein of silk to be woven into a rope.

When the rope was finished, Rapunzel would use it to climb down and escape from the tower. And so for many days they met in secret, and the silken rope grew. One day, however, as Rapunzel was pulling the witch up into the tower, she said without thinking, "How much heavier than the prince you are!" The witch was furious. She wrapped Rapunzel's braid around her hand and snipped it off. Then she cast the girl out of the tower and abandoned her in the forest.

Soon the prince came to call. When he said, "Rapunzel, Rapunzel, let down your hair," the witch lowered the cut-off braid to him and pulled him up. Imagine the prince's horror when he saw, not the lovely face of Rapunzel, but the mocking face of the witch! He fell back in horror into the thorns below, which pierced his eyes and left them blind.

The prince and Rapunzel each wandered alone for many years. Their clothes became tattered, and they grew pale and lean from hunger. But at last the day came when they wandered into the same part of the forest. Rapunzel saw her prince and ran to him, weeping tears of joy. Two of her tears fell upon his eyes, and suddenly he was blind no more. With great joy he led her back to his castle to become his bride, and all of the people rejoiced at their arrival.

Rumpelstiltskin

There was once a miller who bragged constantly about his daughter. One day as the King was riding by, the miller said loudly, "Your Majesty should see my lovely daughter. Why, she is so clever that I believe she could even turn straw into gold!" "Well, let us see if she can," said the King. He told the miller to bring her to the palace that very day.

The miller's daughter came to the palace and was taken to a room filled with straw. "Turn this straw into gold by tomorrow morning," said the King, "if you care for your life!" The daughter was locked in the room and left all alone. "I do not know how to turn straw into gold!" she cried. "If only my father had not boasted so!" "What will you give me to do it for you?" asked a strange voice. There stood a little man with twinkling eyes. "Why, I'll give you the ring on my finger," she said. "Very well," said the little man. He took the ring and sat down at the spinning wheel. Within a few minutes, the piles of straw had become spools of fine gold thread. Then the man was gone, just as suddenly as he had come.

The King was well pleased the next morning to see the golden spools. "I want you to spin a bit more," he said, and he took her to another straw-filled room, twice as large as the first. When he had locked her inside, the miller's daughter wept angrily. "I shall never be free!" she cried. "Oh yes, you will, with my help," said a familiar voice. The little man had returned. "What will you give me to turn all this straw into gold?" he asked. "The chain from around my neck," she said. The little man took the chain, sat down, and spun all the straw into gold, just as before. Then he disappeared.

The King was delighted to see so many golden spools when he opened the door the next morning, and he was glad to see the pretty miller's daughter as well. He took her to a third straw-filled room, three times as big as the first one. "If you can spin all of this straw into gold by morning," he said, "I will make you my Queen." Then the King left the girl alone once more. If I were Queen, she thought, I would be free of this prison. Suddenly the little man stood before her. "What will you give me to help you once more?" he asked. "I have nothing left to give," she said. "Then you must promise to give me your firstborn child," said the little man. "That is a terrible price to pay!" she cried. But since the little man would accept nothing else, she finally agreed. He quickly spun all the straw into gold, then he disappeared.

The miller's daughter and the King were married and, after a time, a beautiful baby was born to them. One day as the Queen sat rocking her child, the little man suddenly appeared. "I've come for the child," he hissed. "Give it to me!" The Queen held her baby tightly and begged the little man to change his mind. "The child is mine!" he insisted. But the Queen pleaded so that at last he gave in. "If you can guess my name in three days' time," he said, "you may keep your child." Then he was gone.

The Queen sent messengers far and wide, and they brought back many names. When the little man returned the next morning, she tried Balthazar, Alexander, and Fernando. But each time the little man answered, "No, that is not my name." The next day, she tried Sheepshanks, Carrot Top, and Long Beard. But the little man always said, "No, that is not my name!"

The Queen began to fear that she would never guess his name! But that very night, one of her messengers came upon a clearing deep in the forest, where a little man danced around a fire. The messenger hid behind a tree, and this is what he heard:

> "Today I brew, tomorrow I bake,
> And then the fair Queen's child I'll take
> And no one can deny my claim,
> For Rumpelstiltskin is my name!"

The messenger rushed back to tell the Queen.

The next day the little man arrived bright and early. "Your time is almost up!" he said. "Yes," said the Queen, "but I shall try once more to guess your name. Is it Broadbuttons?" "No," said the little man. "Is it Jehosaphat?" "No," he said, "that is not my name!" "Hmmm," said the Queen. "Could it be . . . Rumpelstiltskin?" "The devil told you that!" screamed the little man. He stomped his foot so hard that it went right through the floor. Then he grabbed his other foot and pulled himself in two, and the Queen and her child never feared him again.

Sleeping Beauty

A King and Queen longed for many years to have a child. At last a beautiful baby girl was born to them. To celebrate her birth, they held a great feast. Twelve fairies were invited, and the royal artists prepared twelve plates and twelve silver cups especially for them. On the day of the feast, however, a thirteenth fairy appeared. The King and Queen had forgotten to invite her. When she found no gold plate and no silver cup at her place, she was furious.

One after another, each of the fairies bestowed a wonderful blessing upon the baby princess. They wished for her to have goodness, wisdom, beauty, grace, and many other gifts. But just as the twelfth fairy was going to speak, the uninvited fairy interrupted. "I, too, have a gift for the princess," she announced. "One day she will prick her finger upon the spindle of a spinning wheel—and die!"

The King and Queen and their guests cried, "Oh no!" Quickly, the twelfth fairy spoke. "I still have my gift to give," she said, "and although I cannot undo this evil wish altogether, I can help. The princess shall not die, but only sleep until one who is brave and true shall wake her."

The King hoped to keep his daughter safe from the evil fairy's wish. He ordered all the spinning wheels in the kingdom to be burned. Many years passed. The princess grew to be just as kind, wise, and lovely as the good fairies had said she would be. One day as she was wandering through the castle, she came upon a little room high in a tower. In the room sat an old woman wrapped in a cloak. She was spinning.

"What do you have there?" asked the princess.

"It is a spinning wheel, child," said the old woman.

"I've never seen one before," said the princess.

"Would you like to touch it?" asked the old woman. The princess stretched forth her hand, pricked her finger upon the spindle, and fell down in a deep sleep. The old woman stood, threw off her cloak, and ran away. She was the evil fairy! The good fairies found the princess sleeping beside the spinning wheel, and they knew at once what had happened. They sadly carried her to a beautiful bed and made her comfortable. Then they cast a spell upon the whole castle, causing everyone to fall into a deep sleep with the princess. The cook stirring his stew, the groom brushing the horses, even the King and Queen listening to their councilors—all fell asleep wherever they were. At the same time a strong wall of thorns began to grow all around the castle, which was soon completely hidden.

Many years passed, and stories were told far and wide of the beautiful princess who slept behind the wall of thorns. Knights came from faraway lands to try and rescue her, for they hoped to be rewarded with gold and riches. But all of them failed to break through the wall, and many became trapped in the thorns. But one day, there came riding through the kingdom a good and brave prince who wished only to help the princess. He approached the wall of thorns and raised his sword to slash them. Suddenly, the wall opened up before him. He hurried into the castle, past all the sleeping servants, lords, and ladies, and searched until he found the beautiful princess sleeping upon her royal bed. He drew near and gently kissed her. Her eyes fluttered open, and she smiled. At the same moment, all of the castle awoke.

The prince and princess fell in love and were married amid great rejoicing, and they lived together happily for the rest of their days.

Snow White

Once a Queen had a baby princess with hair as black as ebony, lips as red as blood, and skin as white as snow. She named the baby Snow White.

Snow White's mother died, and the King took a new wife. The new Queen was beautiful, but vain and wicked. Every day she stood before her magic mirror and asked:

> "Mirror, mirror, on the wall
> Who is the fairest one of all?"

The mirror always answered, "You, my queen."

All the while Snow White was growing up to be a good, kind and beautiful young woman. One day the mirror said, "Snow White is the fairest one of all." When the wicked Queen heard this she flew into a rage. She called her hunter to her and said, "Take Snow White into the woods and kill her!"

The hunter took the princess far into the woods, but he could not kill Snow White, because he loved her. He told her to run far away and never to come back to her dangerous stepmother.

Left all alone in the woods, Snow White was sad and frightened. She looked for a place to sleep, and came at last to a small cottage. No one was home, but she opened the door and went in. There she saw a table set with seven plates, seven cups, and seven little chairs. She went upstairs and saw seven little beds. She lay down and fell fast asleep.

Soon the owners of the house came back. They were seven kindly dwarfs. Imagine how surprised they were to find Snow White! When she awoke and told them her story, they promised to hide her from the wicked Queen.

But back at the castle, the mirror told all. The Queen asked:

> "Mirror, mirror on the wall,
> Who is the fairest one of all?"

The mirror answered,

> "Over the hill, in the forest glen,
> Snow White dwells with seven little men."

The Queen was furious. This time she would kill Snow White herself. First she dipped a red, juicy apple in poison. Then she disguised herself as an old peddler woman and took the apple to the house of the seven dwarfs. She tapped on the door and said in a sweet voice, "Won't you try my apples?"

Snow White, who was there all alone, did not recognize the wicked Queen. She looked at the red apple and grew hungry. The old woman held it out to her. She took one bite, and fell down, dead.

The dwarfs were heartbroken when they found her. They built a glass coffin for her to lie in, and they watched over her night and day.

One day a handsome prince came riding by. When he saw the lovely girl who seemed only to be sleeping, he could not take his eyes away. He begged the dwarfs to give Snow White to him, so that he could keep her safe in his castle. At last they agreed and sadly lifted the coffin onto their shoulders.

Then a strange thing happened. The coffin tipped and Snow White was shaken. Out of her mouth fell the piece of poisoned apple. Snow White opened her eyes and smiled.

The prince and Snow White fell in love and were married, and all of the dwarfs came to the wedding.

As for the wicked Queen, some say she fell off a cliff, some say she was struck by lightning, and some say she danced herself to death at Snow White's wedding. But one thing is certain: she never bothered Snow White again, and Snow White and the prince lived happily ever after.

The Three Little Pigs

Once a mother pig sent her three children out into the world to make their own homes. The first little pig built a flimsy house of straw and the second little pig built a rickety house of twigs. But the third little pig built a sturdy house of bricks.

Along came the big, bad wolf. He knocked on the door of the straw house. "Little pig, little pig, let me come in," he said.

The little pig saw him through the window and called out, "Not by the hair of my chinny chin chin!"

The wolf said, "Then I'll huff, and I'll puff, and I'll blow your house in!" So the wolf huffed and puffed and blew down the straw house and ate up the first little pig.

Next the wolf went to the house of twigs. He said, "Little pig, little pig, let me come in." But when he heard the wolf's growly voice, the second little pig refused to open the door. The wolf huffed and puffed again, and down fell the house of twigs. The second little pig was gobbled up too.

Now the wolf knocked at the brick house. "Little pig, little pig, let me come in!"

"Not by the hair of my chinny chin chin!"

"Then I'll huff, and I'll puff, and I'll blow your house in!" The wolf huffed and puffed, and he puffed and he huffed, but he couldn't blow down the strong brick house. He decided to try the chimney instead. When the wise little pig heard him on the roof, he quickly built a hot fire in the fireplace. The wolf landed in the fire and was burned so badly that he ran away for good, leaving the little pig to live in peace.

The Ugly Duckling

One warm spring morning, a duck sat patiently upon her egg. Suddenly the egg began to crack open and out came a large, gray duckling with a long neck. "What an ugly baby!" said some of the ducks. They were surprised that he could swim at all.

As the days went by, the mother duck had to protect her big, gray baby from the other ducks. "He's not one of us," they said. Sometimes they even pecked him or chased him. His mother tried to comfort him, but he felt sad and lonely. At last he ran away from the barnyard.

He wandered to the marsh, where the wild ducks and geese lived. At first he feared that they would drive him away, but they paid him little attention. All alone now, he paddled about looking for food.

One day a loud noise rang through the marsh. Hunters were shooting at the geese! The duckling was frightened and tried to hide himself in the weeds. Suddenly a big dog burst into his hiding place. The duckling was sure the dog would attack him, but the dog only stared at him, then walked away. For once I am glad I am ugly, thought the duckling. Even the dog ran from me.

Autumn came, and the leaves turned red and gold, then fell from the trees. The days grew shorter, and the air was colder. One day a flock of snow-white birds with long necks flew over the marsh, heading south for the winter. When the duckling saw them, he thought sadly of his own ugliness and was filled with longing. "If only I could be one of those graceful white birds and fly away with them!" he cried.

As autumn became winter, the duckling shivered with the cold. The marsh was frozen in so many places that he could barely find enough water for swimming, and finally one day his legs froze in the ice beneath him. A farmer

found him, broke away the ice, and carried him to his cozy house to get warm by the fire. Soon the duckling revived. But, afraid of the farmer's family, he ran away. For the rest of the winter he hid in the barn, eating whatever scraps he could find.

At last the air began to grow warmer. It was springtime again, a whole year since the duckling had hatched. How miserable his life had been! He found his way to the marsh and began swimming, all alone. Suddenly he saw several of the beautiful, snow-white birds that had flown past in autumn. They began swimming toward him. They are coming to chase me away, he thought sadly. The white birds drew closer. Were they going to peck him? Slowly they stretched their necks toward him. But instead of pecking, they began to touch him gently. The duckling felt that his heart would burst with happiness.

Then he happened to look down into the water at his own reflection, and he was amazed. For instead of an ugly duckling, he saw a snow-white bird with a long, graceful neck, just as beautiful as the rest. The farmer's children were standing on the bank. "Look!" the little girl cried. "The swans are back, and see—the one Papa saved last winter is with them."

> Many of the stories here come from books by Hans Christian Andersen and the Brothers Grimm. You can find these books in a library or a bookstore if you would like to read longer versions of your favorites.

Why the Owl Has Big Eyes
(AN IROQUOIS TALE)

Raweno, the spirit who makes everything, was busy creating animals. This afternoon, he was working on Rabbit. "May I have nice long legs and long ears like a deer?" Rabbit asked. "And sharp fangs and claws like a panther?"

"Certainly," Raweno said. But he had gotten no farther than shaping Rabbit's hind legs when he was interrupted by Owl.

"Whoo, whoo. I want a nice long neck like Swan's," Owl demanded. "And beautiful red feathers like Cardinal's, and a long beak like Egret's, and a royal crown of plumes like Heron's. I want you to make me into the swiftest and the most beautiful of all birds."

"Be quiet," Raweno said. "You know that no one is supposed to watch me at work. Turn around, and close your eyes!"

Raweno shaped Rabbit's ears, long and alert, just like Deer's.

"Whoo, whoo," Owl said. "Nobody can forbid me to watch. I won't turn around and I certainly won't close my eyes. I like watching, and watch I will."

Then Raweno became angry. Forgetting Rabbit's front legs, he grabbed Owl from his branch and shook him with all his might. Owl's eyes grew big and round with fright. Raweno pushed down on Owl's head and pulled up on his ears until they stood up on both sides of his head.

"There!" Raweno said. "Now you have ears that are big enough to listen when someone tells you what to do, and a short neck that won't let you crane your head to watch things you shouldn't watch. And your eyes are big, but you can use them only at night—not during the day when I am working. And finally, as punishment for your disobedience, your feathers won't be red like Cardinal's, but ugly and gray, like this." And he rubbed Owl all over with mud.

Then he turned back to finish Rabbit. But where was he? Poor Rabbit had been so frightened by Raweno's anger that he had fled, unfinished. To this day, Rabbit must hop about on his uneven legs, and he has remained frightened, for he never received the fangs and claws he had requested. As for Owl, he remained as Raweno shaped him in his anger—with big eyes, a short neck, big ears, and the ability to see only at night, when Raweno isn't working.

What Are Fables?

Most fables are stories that have animals in them, and the animals walk, talk, and act like people. In fact, the animals behave just as well and as badly as people do. Can you guess why? The truth is that fables are really about people.

The most famous fables were said to be told by a man named Aesop ("ee-sop") who lived in Greece long ago. Aesop knew bad behavior when he saw it, and he wanted people to be better, but he knew that we don't like to be told we are bad. So he pretended that many of his stories were about *animals,* not people. His animal characters did all of the things people do that can get them into trouble. They lied and cheated, and were lazy. At the end of the story, Aesop gave people the moral for the story, which was the lesson they should learn.

Here are some fables by Aesop. Can you guess the moral of the story before you read the moral at the end?

FROM AESOP'S FABLES

The Boy Who Cried Wolf

There was once a shepherd boy who watched over a flock of sheep eating grass in the fields. Nearby in the woods lived a wolf that could eat the sheep. Alone all day with no company, the boy grew bored. So one day, he decided to play a joke. "Wolf! Wolf!" he cried, and the villagers came running with their pitchforks to protect the sheep. The boy laughed at the worried villagers, which made them even angrier than discovering his call was a joke. The angry villagers warned the boy that his joke was not funny and went back to their work.

But the boy did not learn. He liked his joke so much that he played it again. Again the villagers came running with their pitchforks to protect the sheep. And again the boy laughed in their worried faces. The villagers warned the boy not to call for help when he did not need help and went back to work.

One day, a big wolf really did attack the sheep. Panicked, the boy cried, "Wolf! Wolf!" but the villagers would not be fooled again. This time they went on with their work, paying no attention to the boy's cries. The wolf killed many sheep, and the boy was ashamed. He finally learned never to cry "wolf"—unless a real wolf was there.

MORAL: "If you often lie, or falsely cry "wolf," people won't believe you even when you are telling the truth."

The Dog in the Manger

On hot days a dog liked to take cover in the manger, which was a long wooden box where hay was put for the farm animals to eat. Finding a bed of cool, dry hay in the manger, the dog fell asleep. Later that day, when the sun went down and the ox had finished pulling the plow, she returned to the manger, hungry for her dinner. But the dog was lying on her hay. "Excuse me," she asked politely, "would you please move over so that I can eat my hay?" Furious at being awakened, the dog growled and refused to budge.

"Please," said the ox. "I haven't had a bite to eat today. If you won't move, I'll go hungry." But the dog, who had no use for the hay, only snapped at her. At last, the weary ox had to give up, and went away tired and hungry.

MORAL: "Don't be mean and grouchy and stingy when you have no need of things yourself. Don't be a dog in the manger."

The Wolf in Sheep's Clothing

Each night, a wolf prowled around a flock of sheep looking for one to eat, and each night the shepherd and his dogs chased him away. Tired of losing out, the wolf thought that there must be an easier way to get his meal. One morning, when he was walking through the woods, he discovered the skin of a sheep. Carefully, he pulled the sheep's skin over him so that none of his fur showed beneath the white fleece. He looked almost exactly like a sheep! The wolf slipped into the flock, and a lamb, thinking that the wolf was his mother, followed him into the woods. When the wolf was sure the shepherd wasn't watching, he cornered the little lamb—and ate him! Pleased that his plan had worked, the wolf went back into the flock the very next night to find a fatter lamb for his dinner. But an odd thing happened. The shepherd decided that he too wanted a sheep for his meal. Taking his knife, he chose the fattest sheep in the flock and slaughtered him on the spot. Guess who it was! The wolf!

TWO MORALS: (1) "Beware of a wolf in sheep's clothing; watch out for those who seem like friends but who might be enemies." And (2) "If you pretend to be what you're not, you might get caught."

The Maid and the Milk Pail

Peggy was a milk maid who had learned to carry heavy things on her head. One early morning, she set out for market with a pail of fresh sweet milk balanced on her head. She was supposed to sell the milk and bring back the pail. As she walked along the road, she thought, with the money I make for this milk I can buy some of Farmer Brown's fat hens. The hens will lay fresh eggs. And those eggs will hatch more chickens. Then, I will wait for winter, when chicken prices are high, and I'll sell them for a very high price. They will fetch enough money for me to buy the blue dress I have wanted, and some blue ribbon to match! I will look so beautiful that all of the boys will want to dance with me at the country fair, and all of the girls will be green with envy. But I won't care. I'll just toss my head at them—like this! And guess what she did. Forgetting all about the pail of milk, Peggy tossed her head, and the white fresh milk spilled and disappeared into the dirt road. Peggy had nothing to sell at market. Ashamed, she returned home empty-handed and told her mother the whole story. Her mother hugged her and said, "Don't count your chickens before they're hatched!"

MORAL: "Don't count your chickens before they are hatched." Have you heard this saying before? It means don't count on things happening the way you want, because you may be disappointed.

The Fox and the Grapes

One hot afternoon, a hungry fox was walking in a vineyard, when he spotted a bunch of grapes hanging high up on a vine. The grapes were so fat with sweet juice that their swaying set the whole vine into motion. But as the fox looked at them hungrily, he realized that the grapes were too high for him to reach. He trotted back a few steps, then ran, and jumped, and missed! He tried again and again, but had no luck. At last, discouraged, he walked away, muttering. "I didn't want them anyway—those grapes were probably sour."

MORAL: "Some people pretend that good things are bad just because they can't have them. When people do this we say, "It's just 'sour grapes.'""

The Hare and the Tortoise

The hare was always boasting that he was one of the fastest animals around, and he enjoyed making fun of the tortoise, because she moved slowly. One day, the tortoise said, "You might laugh at me, but if we raced, I might beat you. Let's race to the main road." The hare agreed, and the race began. The hare started off at top speed and soon left the tortoise far behind. Confident that he would win, the lazy hare decided to nap by the side of the road. He knew that he could overtake the tortoise any time. Meanwhile, the tortoise kept up a slow, steady pace, and the other animals cheered her on. When the hare awoke, he discovered that he had overslept, and the tortoise was waiting for him at the finish line.

MORAL: "Being the most talented doesn't always mean that you'll come out on top. Hard work is more important. Slow and steady wins the race."

The Goose and the Golden Eggs

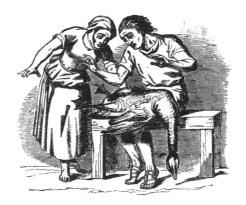

One morning, a farmer discovered that his goose had laid a golden egg. Because the egg was heavier than anything he had seen, the farmer was sure that someone had played a trick on him. But at the market, he proved that the egg truly was made of gold, and he sold it for a small fortune. Every morning thereafter, he discovered and sold another golden egg, and soon he was a rich man. One day, he thought, Why should I wait to grow rich day by day when I could take all of her eggs and be rich in an instant? So he killed his treasured goose, cut her open, and found—no eggs. His dead goose looked just like any other.

MORAL: "When you want something, be patient. If you're greedy, you might lose what you already have, and kill the goose that laid the golden eggs."

Myths and Other Stories

Myths and Legends

Throughout the world, people have told stories that explain the mysterious and powerful things we find in the world, like thunder and rain, and why it gets cold in the winter, and why the stars shine at night. These stories are called myths. Some people used to believe that thunder was caused by a god named Thor. According to them, Thor made the thunder by pounding a mighty hammer. That isn't *really* what makes thunder. The old myths usually aren't true stories, but they provided answers that people believed for a long time.

Legends are about people who are very strong or have magic powers, which they use to defeat monsters and other enemies. Legends usually aren't true, either. Like fables and other stories, myths and legends help us understand our feelings—what we hope for, and what we are afraid of.

Fairies, Elves, Leprechauns, Trolls

Fairy tales, like "Cinderella," are often about fairies or elves. Fairies are usually good, but little elves sometimes play naughty tricks. Good elves do help Santa Claus at the North Pole, but some of them cause mischief. If you can catch an elf called a leprechaun he can show you the pot of gold at the end of the rainbow! A troll can be small like an elf or big like a giant, and is usually very wicked. In this section we will tell you myths, legends, and stories from different countries around the world. The first one is about a troll.

A Troll Story: The Three Billy Goats Gruff

Once there were three billy goats named Gruff who loved to eat fresh green grass. When they had eaten all the grass on their own hillside, they looked longingly at the lush, green hill across the stream. But they were afraid to cross the bridge over the stream for under the bridge lived a mean, hungry troll. This troll was just waiting for a little goat to come along, so he could gobble him up! Finally one day, the youngest billy goat headed for the bridge.

"Trip, trap! Trip, trap!" went the bridge as the youngest billy goat walked across.

"Who's that trip trapping over my bridge?" roared the troll, raising one eyelid, and gazing up through the cracks in the bridge.

"It's me, L-L-Little Billy Goat Gruff," said the youngest goat.

"Sounds like lunch to me," said the troll. And he opened his mouth wide.

"No, please," said the young goat Gruff, scared for his life, "my brother is coming along any minute now. He'd make a much better dinner!"

"Well then," said the troll, who was very lazy and very greedy, "get along with you." So the youngest goat ran as fast as he could across the bridge.

When the second goat saw his little brother eating fresh grass, he wanted some too, so he started across the bridge.

"Trip, trap! Trip, trap!" went the bridge, as he walked across.

"Who's trip trapping over my bridge?" roared the troll.

"It's m-m-me, Middle Billy Goat Gruff," said the frightened goat.

"I thought you'd be along," said the troll. He opened his mouth wide.

"No, wait," said the goat, "there's an even bigger goat coming along, my brother Big Billy Goat Gruff."

"Well," said the troll, "move along." And the goat did, very quickly.

Soon the third goat stepped onto the bridge. "TRIP, TRAP! TRIP, TRAP!" went the bridge.

This must be the biggest goat, thought the greedy old troll, hearing the great noise. "This really *is* my dinner!" And with a single bound, the troll leaped onto the bridge.

Oh, the goat he found there was bigger all right. He was a huge, gruff old goat with a long beard and two great big horns. With a single butt of his head Big Billy Goat Gruff knocked the troll off the bridge and into the waters below. Then he joined his brothers on the hillside, where they all ate so much they were scarcely able to walk home again.

The Legend of Oedipus and the Sphinx

The Sphinx was a strange creature with the body of a lion, the face of woman, and wings to fly.

A long time ago there was a fine city in Greece called Thebes. But the city was being attacked by a Sphinx, who would crouch on top of a large rock beside the main road to the city. And when travelers passed by, the Sphinx would swoop down and pounce on them. Once she had trapped them, she would pose them a riddle. If the travelers could solve the riddle, the Sphinx would let them pass—otherwise the monster would eat them! No one could solve the riddle, and so everyone lived in fear.

One day a young prince named Oedipus came to Thebes from another city. The Sphinx was lying in wait for him. When Oedipus came to the great rock, the Sphinx swooped down and pounced on him. She posed him this riddle: "What creature goes on four feet in the morning, on two feet at noon, and on three feet in the evening?" Now, the Sphinx was very proud of this riddle, and was sure that no one could solve it. She smiled, because she was sure she would have Oedipus for lunch!

Can you help Oedipus solve the riddle? We'll give you a hint. "In the morning," means in the early part of life, "at noon" means in the middle part, and "in the evening" means at the end. This is a very difficult riddle—one of the most famous riddles of all time. Can you think what creature goes on four feet at first, then on two feet, and then on three feet when they're old?

Oedipus smiled at the Sphinx, and said: "Human beings. At first they walk on their hands and knees, which is like walking on four feet. Then they walk standing up, on two feet. And when they're old, they use a cane, which is like walking on three feet." And he solved the riddle!

The Sphinx was so upset that someone had solved the riddle, that she threw herself into the ocean and drowned.

And so Oedipus saved the city from the terrible Sphinx, and the people gave him their queen to marry, and made him king.

The Legend of the Minotaur, Daedalus, and Icarus

The island of Crete in Greece was ruled by a king called Minos. On the island lived a monster called the Minotaur, who was half-man and half-bull. The Minotaur went around eating anyone it could find, so the people of Crete lived in fear.

King Minos went to a clever craftsman named Daedalus, and asked him to help against the Minotaur. Daedalus built a maze called "the Labyrinth." A maze is a very complicated system of passages separated by high walls, and is very hard to escape from. The Minotaur was trapped in the maze and could not escape.

King Minos was very pleased with the Labyrinth, and warned Daedalus never to tell anyone its secret. But Daedalus was proud of his maze, and told others of his accomplishment. He even told someone how you can find your way back out of the Labyrinth once you've gone in.

Can you think of a way of keeping track of where you've been in the maze, so you can come out again?

Here's how Daedalus did it. He left a string behind him as he went. Then, when he wanted to find his way out again, he followed the string!

And so King Minos became angry that Daedalus told others the secret. He shut Daedalus and his son Icarus up in the Labyrinth and blocked the only exit with a great stone.

But Daedalus was very clever. He said to Icarus: "Now there is only one way out. Up, through the air." And so he built himself and his son wings, made of feathers and wax. Then he warned Icarus: "Do not fly too high, or you will fly near the hot sun, and the wax on your wings will melt, and you will fall."

Daedalus and Icarus flew up out of the Labyrinth, and over the sea, and away from the island of Crete. The people looked up at them amazed, as though they were gods or angels.

But Icarus was so proud of his wings that he flew higher and higher. He paid no attention to what his father had told him. He flew so high that the hot sun melted the wax, and his wings came off, and Icarus fell into the sea and drowned. Daedalus was very sad as he looked down at the sea below, and after he landed he never flew again.

The Fable of Brer Rabbit and the Tar Baby

July was a scorcher, and there was not a drop of cool water to be found. Brer Fox, Brer Bear, Brer Skunk, and Brer Possum set themselves to building a water hole. It was hard work, so they made a rule: no one could drink from the well who didn't help build it.

Well, Brer Rabbit didn't lift a finger. He watched them dig and haul, dig and haul, while he sat idle. When the well was finished, Brer Fox warned him, "Lazy Rabbit, don't you take one sip of our water."

But sure enough the well began to run low. Someone was stealing their water, and Brer Fox suspected it was Brer Rabbit, who was always causing trouble. Brer Fox was determined to get Brer Rabbit this time, so he took some black, sticky tar and shaped it to look like a baby. Then he sat it down by the side of the road, and hid in the bushes nearby to watch. Along came Brer Rabbit, just as sassy as you please.

"Good mornin'," he said to the tar baby. Tar Baby didn't say a thing.

"I said 'Good mornin'','" said Brer Rabbit. "Ain't you gonna speak?" Tar Baby said nothing.

Brer Fox lay low in the bushes. "If you don't speak to me," said Brer Rabbit, "I'm gonna bust you wide open!" Tar Baby said nothing, so Brer Rabbit reared back and let the tar baby have it with his right paw. His paw stuck tight! Brer Fox lay low in the bushes. When Brer Rabbit saw that he was stuck, he got madder. "If you don't let go of me, I'll bust you wide open!" he said again. Tar Baby didn't say a thing, so Brer Rabbit let him have it with his left paw, and it stuck tight, too. Brer Fox lay low. Now Brer Rabbit was really mad. "If you don't let me go, I'll kick the stuffin' out of you!" So Brer Rabbit kicked the tar baby first with his right, then with his left foot, and finally butted him with his head. All stuck fast in the tar.

Brer Fox came out of the bushes, laughing. "Well, it looks like I've caught you this time," he said. "Yes, it sure does," said Brer Rabbit. "And I know that after all the tricks I've played on you, you're probably gonna do something terrible to me. But please, oh please, don't throw me in the brier patch! You can shoot me, or fry me, or drop me off a mountain. Just don't throw me in the brier patch!" Now Brer Fox wanted to pay back Brer Rabbit's trickery in the meanest way he could. So in spite of all that begging, he flung him straight into the brier patch. For a long time things got quiet, then Brer Fox heard a sound far away. He looked around to see what it was—and he couldn't believe his eyes! Way up on the top of a hill, there was Brer Rabbit singing and dancing, just as happy as you please. "I was born and raised in the brier patch!" sang Brer Rabbit, "I was born and raised in the brier patch!"

Introduction to Language and Literature

FOR PARENTS AND TEACHERS

There is a character in a Molière play who suddenly discovers that he has been speaking prose all his life. Experts say that our children already know more about the grammar of language than we can ever teach them. But *written* language does have special characteristics that need to be talked about with children. They need to learn the special conventions of written language.

Perhaps the knowledge in this little section isn't as fascinating as stories, but it's needed to help you communicate with young children about language arts. It provides them with a vocabulary to talk about reading and writing.

We have tried to make the information clear. To make it really interesting, the child needs you. Such activities as asking questions, seeking new examples together, praising right answers, and playing guessing games will liven up the proceedings.

Learning About Language

Words and Letters

Language is what we use to say things to each other, out loud or written down. Birds sing, wolves howl, dogs bark, cats meow, but they don't use words. We do. We use them to describe what we see, and hear, and feel. We use words to tell other people what we think.

When words are written down, they are made of smaller parts added together. These parts are called letters.

There are two kinds of letters, vowels and consonants. Vowels are the letters you say with your lips open. They are the "oo" sound in "boo" and the "ee" sound in "eek." They are the "oh" sound in "slow." In English we have five vowels: a, e, i, o, u. That's not many, but you'll find vowels in every word you see. Can you find the vowels in your name?

The other letters in your name are consonants. There are twenty-one consonants in our alphabet. They are the letters that you make with your tongue or your throat or your lips. Listen to the "t" in "town" and "cat." Listen to "m" in "murmur" and "marble." Listen to "p" in "puppet" and "maple." How many consonant letters do you have in your name?

Vowels and consonants are the only two kinds of letters in the alphabet. Remember the alphabet? Let's run through it: a, b, c, d, e, f, g, h, i, j, k, l, m, n, o, p, q, r, s, t, u, v, w, x, y, z. You can mix these letters up in any number of ways to spell every single word in our language, from "supercalifragilistic" to "you" and "me."

ABCDEFGHI
JKLMNOPQR
STUVWXYZ

abcdefghijklmn
opqrstuvwxyz &
1234567890

Small Letters and Capital Letters

Every letter in the alphabet has a big shape and little shape. The big shapes look like this:

A, B, C, D, E, F, G, H, I, J, K, L, M, N, O, P, Q, R, S, T, U, V, W, X, Y, Z,

and we call them capital letters and uppercase letters. But when letters are small we say they are lowercase letters. They look like this:

a, b, c, d, e, f, g, h, i, j, k, l, m, n, o, p, q, r, s, t, u, v, w, x, y, z.

Capital letters at the start of a word say, "This is a new sentence," or, "This word is a name." That's why your name always starts with a capital letter, and the place you live, and the nicknames you have for your friends, and the titles we have for people like Queen Elizabeth I and President Lincoln and Chief Tecumseh.

The Letter

S

The letter "s" has a very important job in telling whether words are singular or plural. Singular means that there is just one. Plural means that there are more than one. Putting an "s" at the ends of some words makes them plural. We have one head, but two eyes and two legs. There is one horse, but several horses.

Sentences and Paragraphs

Sometimes a single word says all you want to say. When you say "Yuck!" you need say no more. Just the one word "sorry" can say a lot, too. But most of the time, we need more than one word to say what we mean; so, we link words together to form a sentence. If you say out loud what you want to do after school tomorrow, you'll probably say a sentence. Here's an example: "I want to go to Tom's house to play." A written sentence starts out with a capital letter that says, "Hey, a new sentence is starting." A sentence ends with a . or ! or ? that says "That's the end."

When we need to say more than a sentence in writing, we use a paragraph. A paragraph is made of several sentences that talk about the same thing.

Punctuation Marks

Punctuation marks are the little signs like ! or . or ? that help us understand a sentence, and tell us how we should read it out loud. When we talk, we use our voices and faces and hands to show what we mean. But when we write and read, we use punctuation marks. They tell you when to raise your voice, and lower it, when to speed up, and when to slow down.

There are three punctuation marks that we use at the end of sentences, so we sometimes call them endmarks. The most used is a little dot like this (.) We call this dot a period.

A question mark (?) looks like a period with a hook on top. When we ask questions out loud, our voices loop up. So, we put question marks on the end of sentences that ask something, such as "How far away is the moon?"

An exclamation point (!) shoots straight up like a rocket taking off, and that's what your voice does when you read it. So we use it to show that we're excited, as in "Wow! I just slam-dunked the basketball!" or "We saw the best movie!"

Wow

We use commas in the middle of sentences. In a long sentence, a comma (,) tells you to slow down, and then keep reading. It also signals a list of things, so instead of writing, "I saw sharks *and* eels *and* manta rays," you could write, "I saw sharks, eels, and manta rays."

Apostrophes (') show where letters are left out. Instead of writing "do not," you can just say "don't." The apostrophe shows where the missing letter belonged. Do you see which letter is missing?

The short word made with an apostrophe is called a contraction. You probably use contractions all the time. Instead of saying "it is," you could just say "it's." Instead of "cannot" you could just say "can't."

When you use an apostrophe with the letter "s" it looks like this: John's book. It shows that a person owns something. Instead of saying, "This is the lizard that belongs to my friend," you could say, "This is my friend's lizard."

Parentheses ( ) look the way your hands do when you cup them together to tell a secret. They let you put a new idea into a sentence. You could say, "When I went trick or treating over Halloween, I got a chocolate bar (my favorite), apples (ugh!), and a squirt gun."

Ugh!

Learning About Literature

Prose and Rhyme

There are many ways to tell a story, but no matter how we tell it, there are only two kinds of language we use—prose and poetry.

Most often, we use prose, which is the kind of language you use when you talk to your friends or tell a joke. Rhyme is used mostly for poems, and you will know it because rhyme words sound alike. Take a word like "feel." It rhymes with "peel," "heel," "deal," "squeal," not to mention "real," "keel," "meal," and "seal."

Listen to this nursery rhyme:

> Hey, diddle, diddle,
> The cat and the fiddle,
> The cow jumped over the moon;
> The little dog laughed
> To see such sport,
> And the dish ran away with the spoon.

Can you find the rhymes? They have the sounds that repeat like the -iddle in "Hey, diddle, diddle, the cat and fiddle" and the -oon in "moon" and "spoon."

Not all poems use rhyme. For instance, here's a poem without it:

> Up and down.
> And round about.
> Back and forth
> And outside in.

Can you turn that into a poem that rhymes?

Heroes and Heroines and Other Characters

Heroes and heroines are the main characters in a story because they are the most brave, or the most kind, or the most of *anything* that is good. When that character is a boy or man, we call him a hero; when it's a girl or woman, we call her a heroine.

All characters aren't heroes and heroines. They can be villains like the puppet master in "Pinocchio" or they can be like normal people you know: mothers, fathers, teachers, fire fighters, children.

Characters don't even have to be people. They can be bears or rabbits, witches or giants. Do you have some favorite characters that aren't people?

Introduction to Sayings

FOR PARENTS AND TEACHERS

Every culture has phrases and proverbs that make no sense when carried over literally into another culture. For many children, this section may not be needed; they will have picked up these sayings by hearing them at home and among their friends. But the category of sayings in the core-knowledge sequence has been the one most singled out for gratitude by teachers who work with children from home cultures that are different from the standard culture of literate American English.

We chose the most common simple sayings and phrases to include in the first book.

SAYINGS AND PHRASES

A.M. and P.M.

People use the abbreviations A.M. and P.M. to help them refer to the time clearly. In America we have two twelve-hour cycles of hours every day. That is, we say 9 o'clock (or 10 o'clock or 11 o'clock) twice each day, once in the morning and once at night. So, to let people know which 9 o'clock we are talking about we say 9 A.M. in the morning and 9 P.M. in the evening. A.M. is an abbreviation for the Latin words ante meridiem, meaning "before noon," and P.M. is an abbreviation for the Latin words post meridiem, which means "after noon." For all the times of the day from 12 midnight until noon, we use A.M., and for all the times between noon and midnight we use P.M. For example, you might go to school at 8:30 A.M. and eat lunch at 12:01 P.M. and get out of school at 3 P.M.

An apple a day keeps the doctor away

People use this saying to mean: eating apples helps keep you healthy. When she unpacked her lunch, Janet groaned, "An apple again!" "But that's good," said her friend Mae. "An apple a day keeps the doctor away."

April showers bring May flowers

People use this saying to mean that something unpleasant can cause something pleasant to happen, just as spring rains cause flowers to bloom. Bob was really miserable. He had caught chicken pox and he couldn't go to the fair. "Cheer up, Bob," said his mother. "April showers bring May flowers: you have to stay home, but I got you the tyrannosaurus model you've been wanting."

Do unto others as you would have them do unto you

This saying is called the Golden Rule. People use it to mean: treat people as you would like to be treated yourself. It comes from the Bible. "Please stop, Molly," said the baby-sitter. "Would you like Becky to knock down a castle you built? Remember: do unto others as you would have them do unto you."

Fish out of water

Since fish can't breathe out of water, people use this saying to mean that someone is very uncomfortable in a new or unusual situation. "I can't sing in front of all those people. I'm not a performer; I've never even been on a stage. I'd feel like a fish out of water."

Hit the nail on the head

People use this saying to mean something you say or do is just right. When you use a hammer, you have to hit the nail right on its head to make it go in straight. "Kate hit the nail on the head when she said that he was angry because he wasn't invited to the party."

If at first you don't succeed, try, try again

People use this saying to mean: don't give up; keep trying. Peter fell every time he tried the skateboard. "You'll get the hang of it, Pete," said his brother. "If at first you don't succeed, try, try again."

Let the cat out of the bag

People use this expression to mean: to tell something that was meant to be a secret. "Jake let the cat out of the bag: he told Sarah about her surprise party."

The more the merrier

People use this saying to welcome newcomers to a group. They say this because it means: the more people who take part in an activity, the more fun it can be. The house was full of kids playing. Still, when the doorbell rang, Mr. DeNiro opened the door and waved in more children, saying, "Come in, come in, the more the merrier."

Never leave till tomorrow what you can do today

People use this saying to mean: don't put off things you have to do. "Let's clean up in the morning," said Heidi. "Nah," said Tina, "let's clean up now. You know what Grandmom always says, 'Never leave till tomorrow what you can do today.'"

Practice makes perfect

People use this saying to mean: doing something over and over makes you good at it. Lucy liked taking piano lessons. She even liked practicing every day. But she got really tired of hearing her dad remind her to practice by saying, "Practice makes perfect."

Raining cats and dogs

People use this saying to mean that it is raining very, very hard. "I don't want to walk home; I'll get soaked. It's raining cats and dogs!"

There's no place like home

People use this saying to mean: travel may be pleasant, but home is the best place of all. "We had a great trip, but there's no place like home."

Once a child knows some sayings, you might enjoy varying the words playfully. If an apple a day keeps the doctor away, what does a banana do? Cloudy with a Chance of Meatballs *by Judith Barrett (New York: Macmillan Publishing Co., Inc., 1978) does this with an extravagance children love.*

II.

GEOGRAPHY, WORLD CIVILIZATION, AND AMERICAN CIVILIZATION

Introduction to Geography

Americans of past decades, living in a large and relatively self-sufficient country, have had little incentive to gain geographical knowledge about the world that lies beyond North America. When the Korean and Vietnam wars began, few of us knew where Korea and Vietnam were to be found. As I write, American men and women are fighting a war in a part of the world called "the Middle East," which is for many of us a geographically fuzzy concept. And our children tend to know even less about geography than we do. According to a study prepared by the National Geographic Society in 1988, our children are perhaps the only children in the world who know less geography than their parents do. This continuing and deepening American tradition of geographical vagueness, while understandable, has never been admirable, and is much harder to justify now that we participate in political and economic affairs that are increasingly global in character.

Unquestionably, the elementary school years are the best years to gain a permanent familiarity with the main features of world geography—the continents, the larger countries, the major rivers and mountains, and the major cities of the entire world. These spatial forms and relationships, when properly learned and connected with interesting stories, will remain unforgettable, as everyone who has had good early schooling in geography will attest. Later on, as geographical understanding deepens, those early images become more fully correlated in our minds with an understanding of climate, agriculture, history, and culture. But the forms and spatial relationships that are learned early are the ones that remain most securely fixed in our minds. They become familiar and reliable patterns which we carry with us all our lives. They orient us when we encounter references to Sri Lanka or Malaysia or Ethiopia, or when someone asks how can Israel connect with Egypt when Israel is in Asia, and Egypt in Africa?

We would know the answer instantly if we carried a clear mental picture that Asia connects to Africa near the mouth of the Nile.

Such knowledge is gained by consistent mapwork that should include a lot of active drawing and coloring, and place-name identification. The association of shapes with names of places is at least as much fun as pinning the tail on the donkey. Committed teachers testify that the drawing of maps can be as absorbing as the drawing of pictures. Geography is and ought to be fun. But if the sense of the importance of geography is to be adequately conveyed to children, parents and teachers must be themselves convinced of the growing importance of geographical knowledge.

Geography

The Earth: A Huge Ball

Pretend you are standing on the moon. Look toward our world, away from the sun. Now you would see a huge, bluish ball with white clouds around it. From the moon, our earth looks something like that.

This is a view of the earth from the moon.

A Map of the World

Look at the picture of our world on page 88. We could not put a ball in your book, so we drew a flat picture of it, called a map.

How to Look at a Map

Learning how to look at this map is not hard, but first you have to know the four main directions that tell you where things are. Everything on earth is in a certain direction from where you are right now. If you look at the door of your room, you are looking in the direction of the door. Do you know the four main directions? They are east, west, north, and south. Let's find those directions from where you are right now.

East is near where the sun rises. If you don't know where that is, you can wait until early tomorrow morning to find out.

West is near where the sun sets. You can find out where that is late today or tomorrow.

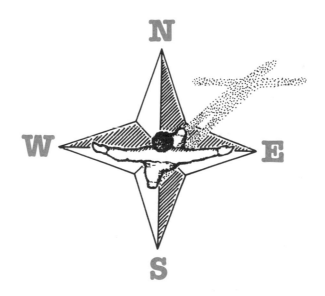

Once you have found out where the sun rises, you can find all the directions. Here's how. Stick your arms straight out from your sides. Slowly turn yourself until your right arm points to where the sun comes up. Can you tell your right arm from your left? Keep those arms straight. Your right arm is now pointing east and your left arm is pointing west. Now keep those arms straight just a minute longer, and look straight ahead. Your nose will be pointing to the north, and the back of your head will be pointing to the south. Now you can put your arms down. What direction is your door? Is it nearest to east, west, north, or south?

Now you can learn quickly how to look at a map. The top of the map is north. The bottom is south. The right is east. The left is west. Left and west sound almost the same; that will help you remember how to look at a map.

Oceans

Now, let's look at the map of the earth. It tells us that most of our world is made up of large spaces of water. They are called oceans. The largest ocean is the Pacific. Can you find it? The next largest is the Atlantic Ocean. Where is it?

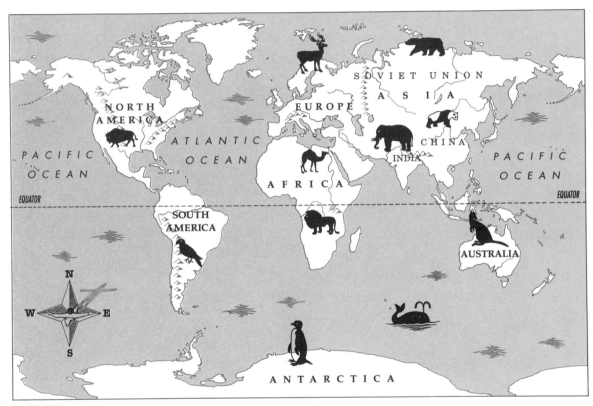

Land

Look at the spaces that are *not* water. That is the land where people live. The seven largest spaces of land are called continents.

The Equator

Before we name the different continents, look at the line in the middle of the map. There is not really a line drawn on our world, but it is put on the map to show the middle of the world, where the climate is hot. The line is called the equator. The people who live near this imaginary line never need a heavy winter coat at all!

The middle of the world is hot, but at the very top and bottom of the world it is very cold. The top and bottom are covered with thick ice. Do you know some special animals that live at the bottom or the top of the world? How about one that looks as if he's borrowed a big, white fur coat or one that looks as if he's rented a tuxedo?

The Continents

Asia

Look again at the seven big pieces of land, called continents. Are they all the same size? No! One is much larger than the others. It is called Asia. It stretches west from the Pacific for thousands of miles. More than one half of all the people in the world live in Asia.

Would you expect the world's largest continent to have the world's largest country? It does. It's the Soviet Union, which is often called Russia. It has more land than any other country. It also has more people than any other country except for two. Do you know which ones they are?

Would you expect the largest continent to have the countries with the most people? It does. China has the most; India is second.

Can you point to where China and India are on the map? Can you find the big Soviet Union?

Would you expect the biggest continent to have the highest mountains? Asia does have the highest mountains in the world. They are located northeast

of India. It is very, very cold at the top of these high mountains, where the snow never melts.

Have you ever seen a panda? It comes from China. Other animals come from Asia, too. Have you ever seen other animals that live in Asia?

Did you know that many people left Asia to come live in our country? Did anyone in your family come from Asia?

Asian tiger.

Europe

Europe is attached to the northwestern part of Asia and stretches west to the Atlantic Ocean. You might not think of Europe as a continent, but the Ural Mountains divide it from Asia. Can you find the Ural Mountains on the map?

Down below Europe, to the south, is the Mediterranean Sea. It is not as large as an ocean, but it is certainly big.

Europe has many mountain chains. Some, like the Alps, have high peaks. Others, like the Urals, are much lower.

Europe is the second-smallest continent, but it has a lot of the world's people. There are many cities and towns in Europe. Many people left Europe because the cities and towns were too crowded. Some came here to our country. Did anyone in your family come from Europe?

There are cold winters in the north of Europe, and hot summers in the south. But in most of Europe the weather does not get very cold or very hot.

Because Europe has so many people, it no longer has many large wild animals. But one kind of wild animal runs free in northern Europe. Santa Claus is supposed to have some of those animals. Can you guess what they are called?

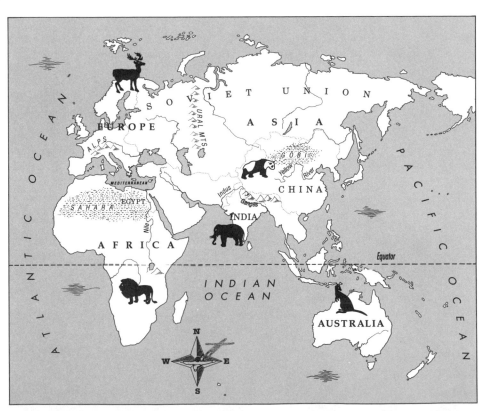

This is a picture of the Sahara Desert.

Africa

Look south (down) from Europe and you will find the second-largest continent, Africa. How long would it take to row a boat across the Mediterranean Sea to get from Europe to Africa? Too long. Don't try it!

The northern part of Africa is nearly all hot, dry desert. A desert is a place that has very little rain. The desert in northern Africa is the largest in the world. It is called the Sahara.

The Sahara is a place of sand hills, rocks, and mountains. Because it has little rainfall, not many plants can grow there.

Only one place in the Sahara has lots of plants. They grow along a river that gives them water. This is the Nile River—the longest river in the world. In Africa, the world's longest river flows through the world's biggest desert.

One animal, the camel, seems to like the Sahara. It has very long eyelashes to keep swirling sand out of its eyes, and it can store enough water to walk a long time in the desert without drinking.

The central part of Africa is often hot, but plants and trees grow well because there are heavy rains that water them. In the forests are wild gorillas, chimpanzees, and monkeys. In the grasslands roam lions, zebras, giraffes, and antelopes. Can you think of other big animals that live in Africa? Don't forget the animals that swim in the lakes and the great rivers of Africa.

The ancestors of many people in our country came from Africa. Most came from western Africa, south of the Sahara. Did anyone in your family come from Africa?

Scientists believe that the first humans developed in Africa over a half million years ago. Gradually, humans spread from Africa all over the world. If these scientists are right, then all of us originally started in Africa, including those whose ancestors later came from Asia and Europe.

Some of the first humans in Africa probably slept in caves. Even in Africa the nights are sometimes cold. Can you imagine you are an early human who sleeps in a cave? What could you sleep on? How would you keep warm? What would you eat?

Y*ou can find pictures of African animals in the* National Geographic World, *a children's magazine. It will be in your school or town library.*

North America

North America is the third-largest continent. It has rivers and mountains, great deserts, and deep canyons. It even has volcanos. It has cold parts and hot parts. Its climate suits the polar bear of the freezing north as well as the parrot of the hot tropics.

Do you know how big a polar bear is? Can you find out what a volcano is? (Hint: it BOOMS hot lava out of its top.)

Polar bears walking on ice.

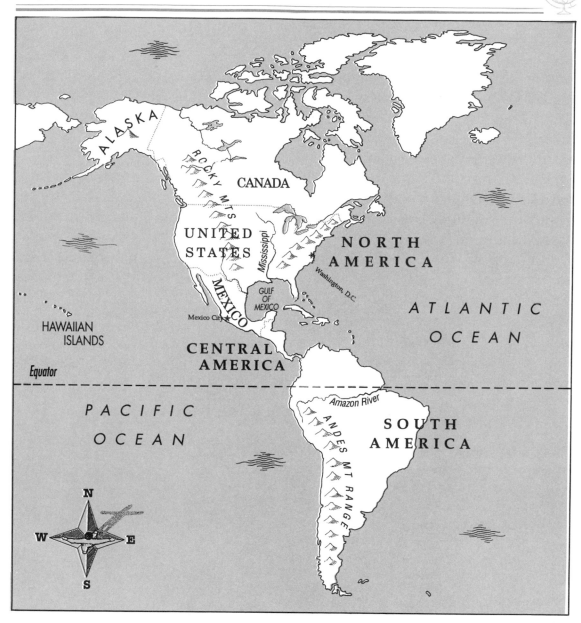

Canada

Can you see from the map that Canada is the largest country in North America? It reaches from the northern border of our country almost to the top of the world.

Since it is a northern country, Canada is cold in the winter.

Thousands of years ago, Canada was covered by ice both in winter *and* in summer. That time was called the Ice Age. The ice came down from the north and spread into the United States, too. It was a huge, thick blanket of ice, called a glacier. When the world got warmer, the ice melted.

United States

The United States of America is the central country in North America. On the west is the Pacific Ocean, and on the east is the Atlantic. Near the middle flows a great river, called the Mississippi, which divides the east from the west. Once, huge herds of buffalo roamed the grasslands west of the Mississippi River. Wolves, bears, and many other animals lived on both sides of the river. But most of these animals have been replaced by millions of people, by us.

We live in sections called states. There are fifty states in our country. Forty-eight are together on both sides of the Mississippi. But two, Alaska and the Hawaiian Islands, are far away. There are also island territories and our capital city, Washington, D.C.

Which state do you live in? What ocean is nearest to our capital, Washington, D.C.?

Mexico and Central America

Mexico is the country south of the United States. Can you find it on the map? Notice how it curves down below the United States. Do you think the weather would be warm in Mexico? Can you say why you think so?

Mexico has mountains and volcanoes and jungles. A big, spotted cat called the jaguar hunts in Mexico.

These people in Guatemala are taking water home from a well.

In Mexico, people speak Spanish. One of the biggest cities in the world is there, and it is easy to remember because it is called "Mexico City."

The earliest cities in North America were in Mexico. They were the cities of some ancient people we will talk about in this book called the Maya and the Aztecs.

Central America is connected to Mexico. You can find it if you keep following Mexico as it curves to become a bridge of land between North America and South America. Do you see the bridge of land? It contains seven small countries that have warm, rainy climates. The people in those countries speak Spanish, just as they do in Mexico.

South America

The fourth-largest continent is South America. It stretches from the tropics above the equator almost to the bottom of the world. The Andes Mountains on the western side of the continent are the longest chain of mountains in the world. They run north to south like a spine, the way your spine runs from your head to your legs!

The Amazon River cuts the South American continent at its widest part as it flows from west to east. It is the second-longest river in the world (after the Nile) and carries the most water of any river in the world. It is a tremendous river! You could spend weeks traveling its length by boat, and part of the time you could be on an oceangoing boat!

The Amazon flows through the largest tropical rain forest in the world. The forest has thousands of kinds of plants and animals—so many that some have not been named yet by scientists.

Antarctica

At the top of the world, there is no land, only frozen ocean. But at the bottom of the world there is a continent called Antarctica. Antarctica is covered with ice that is from one to two miles thick. Sometime when you are taking a walk or even riding in a car, notice how far a mile is. Then imagine how deep this ice is!

Living in Antarctica is like living during an Ice Age. It is so cold in winter that only scientists and exploration groups try to stay there. The summers there are more like our winters!

Can animals live in this intense cold? No! There are no animals that live on the ice. There are many animals, though, that live along the edge of the ice by the sea. There are also many in the waters: penguins, seals, and whales are some of them.

Penguin.

Do you know how one kind of large penguin keeps its egg warm during the cold winter? Huddling with others in a large group, a father penguin holds the egg on top of its feet, tucked under a flap of skin. How amazing that an egg can hatch in such cold!

Australia

The smallest continent is the island of Australia in the South Pacific. It is the only continent that contains just one nation. Partly because so much of it is desert, Australia has the fewest people of all the continents except Antarctica.

Because Australia is so far from all of the other continents, its animals developed without contact with animals from other parts of the world. One strange-looking creature found nowhere else is the kangaroo. It jumps long distances and carries its babies in a pouch. Another Australian animal is the koala bear. It looks very cuddly and eats only the leaves from the Australian gum tree.

N ow that you have finished this book's geography, try naming the continents aloud, in order of size: Asia, Africa, North America, South America, Antarctica, Europe, Australia. How many are there?

What were the names of the two largest oceans? Do you remember the one smaller body of water you learned—the Mediterranean Sea? Where is it?

If you trace pictures of the animals you read about here, you can color them. Then you can put the animal with its continent.

Introduction to World Civilization

In schools the world over, in Asia, Africa, the Americas, Europe, and Australia, young children are learning some of the same things about the history of human civilizations—about Egypt and other African civilizations, about Chinese history, the Babylonians, the Incas, Aztecs, and Maya. Today, perhaps for the first time ever, children on all continents are learning not just the history of *their* ancestors, but also the broader history of all mankind.

This fortunate educational change may help reduce cultural conflict within and among nations. The study of world history is particularly appropriate in the United States where our population has come from every part of the world. To know world history is partly to know ourselves. The great American writer Herman Melville said about the United States:

> Settled by the people of all nations, all nations may claim her for their own. You cannot spill a drop of American blood without spilling the blood of the whole world . . . We are not a nation so much as a world.

The diversity of America is becoming the norm for other nations of the modern world. People from all over are to be found in almost every country, some to find better jobs, others to participate in international business. The modern international economy has turned the whole world into a single marketplace. The new global economy has created a new cosmopolitanism which makes it desirable that children in all countries, and especially in our own culturally diverse one, should share a basic knowledge of world history.

How reassuring it is to know that our children, by studying the larger history of mankind, will learn much the same history as children in other lands. The historical knowledge they will share will cause them to understand that people in every country have a common human heritage and a common stake in fostering a peaceful and civil world.

In this section, children are introduced to what history is, to the colorful Egyptians with their pyramids and mummies, to Babylon with its harsh laws, and to the great religions of the world.

In this section, you will find suggestions for activities that might help make the stories more vivid and memorable. These suggestions, which include recipes, role-playing, and titles of related materials, can also serve as models for other activities you invent yourselves.

World Civilization

Everybody's Story

History is the story of the people who lived before you were born. It tells you about things that happened so long ago even the oldest person in the world today can't remember them. History can be the most exciting and interesting story that you will ever hear!

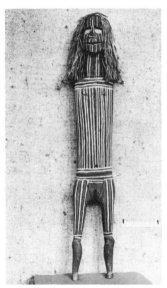

What are some of the first things you remember? Did they happen last year? Two years ago?

If your mother or father or teacher is reading to you, ask about the first event they remember. How many years ago did *that* happen?

Is one of your grandparents reading this to you? Your grandparents can remember further back than your parents. How many years can your grandfather or grandmother remember?

But even your grandparents would have no memory at all of the young King you are going to hear about next. He lived over three thousand years ago! And there were kings before him who lived over five thousand years ago!

The Nile Gives Tut a Present

In the earliest times, people didn't know how to grow their food. Until they learned, they had to hunt wild animals. Even after they gathered animals into flocks and herds, they had to keep moving from one grassland to another to feed them. Sometimes they were lucky and could sleep in caves!

But when people planted food and gathered together into villages they could sleep in strong buildings they made for themselves. One country where

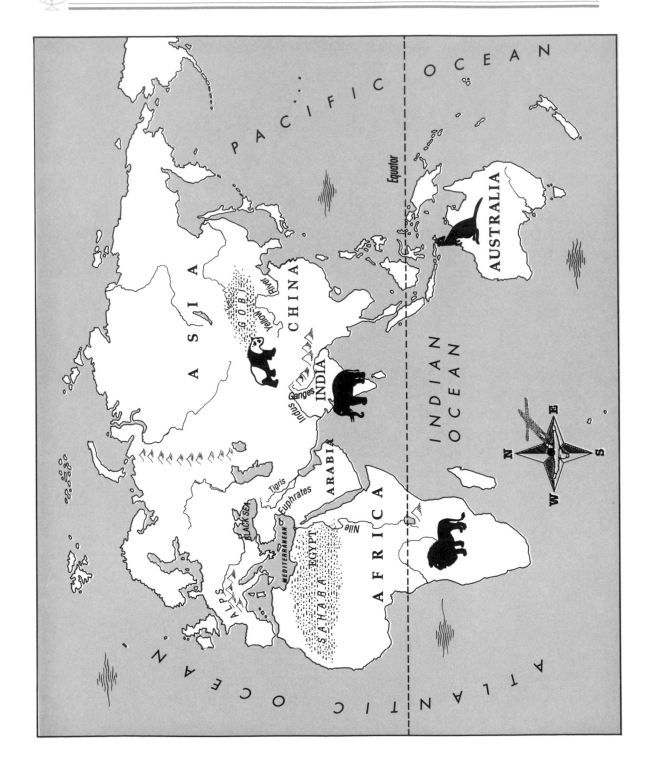

people started growing food crops and building houses was Egypt. You can find Egypt on your map.

There was a king in Egypt who made laws so that people would get along together in the cities. This king was called pharaoh. When one king died another took his place. Sometimes the new king was very young.

One young pharaoh was called Tutankhamen, or King Tut for short. He lived in Egypt beside the longest river in the world, the Nile. Find the Nile on your map.

You can see that the Nile begins in central Africa. It flows northward from high lakes and passes through a great desert. It ends in the Mediterranean Sea. Each year the northern part of the Nile flooded over its banks. That was where Egypt began.

This is a mask that went over King Tut's mummy.

Everything in Ancient Egypt depended on the overflowing of the Nile. The water left rich, moist soil called silt on its banks for ten miles on each side. Ten miles! In the moist, rich soil the farmers planted food crops. Did you ever plant something in good soil and keep it watered? What happened?

Since it is very warm all year in Egypt, the Egyptians could grow a lot of food. The fish and birds of the river also provided food. Being able to grow crops in one place meant that the people no longer had to move around. They could stay and build villages and cities. It was the overflowing Nile that let the Egyptians start their cities. That was the present that the Nile gave King Tut and the Egyptians.

The First Kingdom

Pretend you could visit those ancient times, and that King Tut has asked you to go on his riverboat with him—for crocodile hunting on the Nile. Of course you would accept!

Boats on the Nile.

King Tut doesn't expect you to try to spear the dangerous crocodile. He has servants for that, and you are his guest. So you sip his fruit drink and politely ask a few questions about those gigantic pointed monuments you have seen in the desert. They seem to reach to the sky. You have heard that they are called pyramids.

King Tut is only a teenager himself, so he doesn't remember when the pyramids were built. That was done well over a thousand years before he was born. But he knows the story of the pyramids, because the older Egyptians had invented a language of word pictures, and Tut could read the story about the pharaohs who built the pyramids. But Tut says that the story of the pyramids won't make sense to you unless you first learn about mummies.

What Are Mummies?

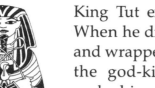

King Tut explains that he is a god-king. When he dies his body must be preserved and wrapped for the journey to the land of the god-kings. Strips of cloth will be soaked in special liquids and wrapped all over his body until he looks like one big bandage. Then he will be a mummy, and can go on his journey. Once he is there he will pray that the gods continue to make Egypt a land where good crops grow and no one starves.

All the earlier pharaohs and queens had been wrapped into mummies, Tut tells you. A few of the earliest rulers had pyramids built so their mummies could be put into them. They hoped to touch the world of the gods. That was the story of why the pyramids were built.

Pyramids.

Tut isn't really sure that's why the pyramids are so high. There are different stories. But everybody agrees about one thing. It took many years and many thousands of people to build the pyramids. And some of these people were slaves. Each pyramid is made of thousands of stones, each stone weighing more than an automobile. The biggest pyramid is almost as high as two football fields are long. The space that it takes up on the ground would cover the space of thirteen football fields. Nobody knows how the Egyptians did it. We do know they had to work hard under the hot sun to cut and move those huge stone blocks, and then pile them high on top of each other.

Animal Gods

After your trip on the Nile, you return to Tut's palace. He gives you several statues made of pottery as going-away presents. They are statues of his favorite gods. They have human bodies, but they have animal heads: a falcon, a ram, a cow, and a crocodile!

You almost shout in surprise. But Tut is a king, so you are very quiet and polite. You thank him for the statues, and ask him about the huge, huge statue you saw near the pyramids. It has a lion's body and a man's head. It is called the Sphinx. Tut tells you it is supposed to represent the pharaoh himself.

King Tut lived three thousand years ago. We know about him because his beautiful treasures were discovered inside the tomb where he was buried. These are now kept in a big building called a museum.

You hurry to the museum to see the treasures, and what sights you see! There is a golden chariot for Tut's journey to the gods. There are chests of gold jewelry, and his mummy case is solid gold. There are cups and combs and food for him to use in the afterlife. Someone even thought to add a statue of a sacred cat to keep the mice away!

In the museum you are back in the present. But you know you will never forget King Tut.

You can read about building the pyramids and see many of King Tut's treasures in a book called Ancient Egypt: Discovering its Splendors *published by the Geographical Society, Washington, D.C., in 1978. And three issues of* National Geographic *magazine also tell you about Tut and Ancient Egypt: October 1963, January 1974, and March 1977.*

A coloring book of ancient Egypt has been published by Dover Publications, 31 East Second Street, Mineola, New York 11501. It is sold at a reasonable price, and the pictures can be reproduced without paying a copyright fee.

Babylonia: Another Gift

East of Egypt there were *two* rivers that flooded. Like the Nile, these rivers gave the gift of rich soil and plentiful food. A city grew up called Babylon. (The names of the two rivers are the Tigris and the Euphrates, but you only need to remember the name Babylon now.)

The Babylonians invented a different kind of writing from the Egyptians. When we figured out how to read it, we discovered the name of their king, Hammurabi. We discovered a set of laws he made. Some of these laws seem cruel to us. One law said that if a son hit his father, his hand was to be cut off! Another law seems much more fair: a physician was supposed to charge a poor man less than a rich man.

Babylon was strong for a while. But the Babylonians did not use horses in battle, and they lost their city to invaders who did. Why do you think riding a horse was so important?

Judaism

More than a thousand years after Hammurabi, Babylon was still a rich city. Her rulers at that time conquered nearby people. One group of people that they conquered were called the Jews. The Jews did not believe in many gods, as the Egyptians and Babylonians did. The Jews believed in one god.

The Egyptians also conquered the Jews. Once, when the Jews had been made slaves in Egypt, the Pharaoh's daughter found a little Jewish baby in a basket beside the Nile. She felt sorry for him and secretly took him into the palace. When he grew up he found out that he was Jewish, not Egyptian. Then he led all the Jews out of Egypt to their homeland, which is now called Israel. His name was Moses. Do you think it was hard for Moses to give up an easy life in the palace?

The escape of the Jews from Egypt is still celebrated as a holiday in the Jewish religion. It is called Passover. An important symbol of the Jewish religion is the Star of David.

Christianity

Many hundreds of years after Moses led the Jews out of Egypt, a group branched out from the Jewish religion. These people were called Christians. The first Christians were Jews who followed the preaching of Jesus of Nazareth. They considered Jesus to be the "Christ," a savior who had been promised to the Jewish people.

Jesus attracted many followers. He taught that people should love God and love their neighbors as much as they love themselves. He said they should even forgive their enemies.

Jesus died on a cross, so a cross has become the main symbol of Christianity. Christians believe that on the third day after Jesus died, he rose from the dead. Christians celebrate Jesus' birthday at Christmas, and his rising from the dead at Easter.

TEACHING THROUGH PARABLES

When Jesus preached to people, he often told parables. A parable is a story that teaches a lesson.

Jesus preached that you should love your neighbor as you love yourself. Once a lawyer asked Jesus, "Who is my neighbor?" To answer this question, Jesus told the parable of the Good Samaritan. (A Samaritan is a person from the region called Samaria. These people were not Jews, and were looked down on by the Jewish people in Jesus' time.)

Once, said Jesus, a man was traveling along the road. Suddenly he was attacked by thieves, who robbed him and beat him. The man lay half-dead by the side of the road. Soon a Jewish priest came along, but he passed the man by. Then another religious man passed by without helping. Then along came a Samaritan. When the Samaritan saw the half-dead man, said Jesus, he "went to him, and bound up his wounds." He took the man to a nearby inn. He told the innkeeper that he would pay whatever it cost to take care of the man.

Then Jesus asked the lawyer, "Which now of these three was neighbor unto him that fell among the thieves?"

Today, people sometimes call anyone who goes out of his or her way to help someone else a "good Samaritan."

Islam

The idea of one god spread from the Jews and the Christians to many sections of the world. Hundreds of years after Jesus lived, a man named Mohammed was born in Arabia. Can you find that on the map?

Mohammed had his wife write his teachings in the Koran and gathered believers to hear them. This angered the leaders of his city, who forced him to leave! He returned many years later to take over Mecca. After that all of Arabia accepted him as a messenger of Allah, their one god. The crescent is the symbol of Islam.

Hinduism

Hinduism is a religion believed in by millions of people in India. It started a long time ago.

Even before Babylon was built, wanderers in Asia had found another river that helped them grow good food crops. This was far to the east, almost as far as India. The river is called the Indus. Look at the map. Do you think people might have gone by boat to the Indus? Where could they have started from?

Gradually, villages spread across India. The people believed in many gods to explain life and nature. They also came to believe in a "great force," called Brahma. These beliefs are called Hinduism, a religion that still exists today.

Buddha: A Young Prince

Another religion of millions of people in Asia is Buddhism. It is based on the teachings of the Buddha.

The man who became the Buddha was the son of a King in the mountains of India. He gave up being a ruler to gain wisdom and become a teacher.

To find his own answers to life he decided to think quietly. It has been said that he sat beneath a tree for ninety-eight days! Don't you think that is a long time to keep quiet?

By the end of ninety-eight days he had become wise or "enlightened." The word "Buddha" means

This is a Chinese carving of Buddha.

"the Enlightened One." He began to teach and many believed him. One of the things Buddha taught is that we should not hurt any living thing. Buddha's teachings spread into a great part of Asia. They are still followed by many people there.

Buddha Stops an Elephant

Buddha had a cousin who did not believe him. In fact, the cousin was so jealous of Buddha's fame that he tried to kill him! One day, the legend says, a wild elephant was prodded by Buddha's cousin. It trumpeted a loud, harsh noise and rushed at Buddha! But Buddha talked calmly to the elephant and instead of crushing him, the elephant knelt down.

Confucius: A Poor Chinese Boy

About the same time that Buddha lived in India, another young man in China was teaching about the best way to live. His name was Confucius.

By his time, China was a large country ruled by an emperor. Civilization had begun in China the same way it had in Egypt and Babylon and India. People had discovered that the Yellow River flooded, leaving rich soil on either side of the river. They could stay in one place and grow food crops. They could build cities.

By the time Confucius lived, China had large buildings, beautiful art, and even silk. Someone had learned to unravel the cocoon of a mulberry tree worm and make silk from it. Have you ever seen a cocoon? Have you ever seen silk?

China was rich, but most of the people were not happy. There was too much fighting about who would be emperor. This wasted China's wealth and kept most of the people poor. Confucius knew that well, because his own family was very poor.

To make China peaceful and happy, Confucius taught the rules of "right living." Peace and wisdom were very important, Confucius said. So was respect for parents. Slowly, these teachings spread across China. People there have believed them for over two thousand years! During much of that time Confucius's rules have helped to keep peace. Confucius's ideas also led to many of China's children being sent to school. Is that good?

Happy New Year

Many traditions still followed in China come from before the time of Confucius. One tradition is that red is a lucky color. Another tradition is the celebration of the Chinese New Year. Many people in this country also celebrate the Chinese New Year. Each new year is given the name of an animal, like a tiger or a dragon. The year of the rabbit is a very lucky year. On the next page we have given some tips about how to celebrate the Chinese New Year.

Now that you have finished world history for this year, here is a question. Why did people in early times start building cities near rivers that flooded?

Let the children pretend they have a friend who celebrates the Chinese New Year. They are asked to join him or her for the fun. They gather with the whole family the night before the new year at their home. First, they help their friends put strips of red paper around the doors. This keeps the family's wealth from escaping. Then they join the prayers before the feast. At midnight they help take the red paper down. This lets in the good spirits of the new year.

Here is the first dish that might be served at the feast. With help, children will enjoy making this. (1) Hard-boil 4 eggs. (2) Leaving them in their shells, roll them around on a hard surface to make the shells crack all over. (3) Keeping the shells on, place the eggs in a pan and cover them with water. (4) Add 2 teaspoons tea leaves, 1 teaspoon sugar, ⅓ teaspoon salt, 1 tablespoon soy sauce. (5) Bring to a boil and simmer gently for 1 hour. Turn the eggs now and then to be sure they are coloring evenly. (6) Let the eggs cool in the pan. (7) When cool, carefully peel the eggs. You will see they look like marbles. (8) Arrange the whole eggs on a plate with slices of cucumber or carrots.

Introduction to American Civilization

FOR PARENTS AND TEACHERS

Changes are afoot in the teaching of social studies. A public outcry has begun against watered-down social studies textbooks whose chief goal has been to avoid offending anyone—even if that should mean removing all vividness and avoiding fundamental facts of history.

The advisory committees for this series decided to include American history in the very earliest grades. Although some schools now wait until grade five to begin a significant study of American history, our best schools have always started earlier. They have proved that children in early grades are fascinated by stories of the American past—stories that go beyond "Why we celebrate Thanksgiving."

Perhaps the most important reason for our decision to start early was our concern for fairness. Knowledge of American history and society is gained through the pores by children from advantaged families. It seemed unfair to our committees that children from less advantaged homes are now being denied basic knowledge which helps children understand the social and intellectual world around them. Social and cultural knowledge are built up gradually. An early, systematic exposure to history provides a framework for fuller understanding later on. It is simply unfair that the possession of such a framework should be determined by chance and luck rather than by good schooling.

In Book I we have told stories about high points of American history from the first settling of the Americas over the Alaskan land bridge to the Louisiana Purchase. Parents and teachers will find suggestions for making the stories more memorable and vivid in activity boxes throughout the chapter.

Good luck in making the teaching and learning of American history great fun!

American Civilization

Legends and Leaders
Who Built The Bridge?

Between Alaska and Asia there is now water. But long ago there was a bridge of land between Alaska and Asia. Can you trace with your finger on the world map where this bridge of land used to be?

The land bridge disappeared about twelve thousand years ago. That's so long ago we can hardly imagine it. The Egyptians probably hadn't even started planting on the banks of the Nile. It was across this bridge that people first came to North and South America.

A Very Long Trip

You remember, scientists say that human beings began in Africa. After a long time, some of them traveled from Africa to Asia. After more time, they came from Asia to America over the land bridge!

The people who came stayed here and over thousands of years the number of people in America grew. They spread all over North and South America. These were the ancestors of the people we now call Native Americans or American Indians.

These people came over the land bridge chasing animal herds. They hunted to eat. For thousands of years, these first Americans were able to keep hunting because there were always so many fish to catch and animals to hunt. They also gathered berries, fruits, and nuts.

But in some of the warmer places in the south, where it is easy to grow plants, the earliest Americans began to grow food crops. The crops gave

them plenty to eat. They didn't have to move and hunt for food. They could stay in one place and develop towns and cities.

Cities in the Jungle: The Maya

Maya pyramid.

One group of these city dwellers lived long ago in the jungles of Central America. These people were called the Maya. They grew corn and beans, and built cities. Their largest buildings were pyramids. Their pyramids were not as high as the ones in Egypt, but they had steps from the bottom to the top for the priests to climb. At the top of the pyramids the Maya worshiped their gods.

We don't know why the Maya left their cities after hundreds of years. The Maya still live in Central America but now the jungle covers their ancient buildings.

National Geographic *published three books about the Aztecs, Incas, and Maya, which can be purchased individually or as a set. They are called:* The Mighty Aztecs, The Mysterious Maya, *and* The Incredible Incas. *The text is for older children, but the pictures will make these ancient civilizations come alive for any age. The phone number for* National Geographic *is (800) 638-4077.*

City on the Lake: The Aztecs

Long after the Maya left their cities, a very fierce people appeared in the area that is present-day Mexico. They were the Aztecs. They conquered the people already there, and ruled over much of Mexico.

The Aztecs built a capital on islands in a lake. Mexico City, one of the largest cities in the world, stands there now.

The Aztec warriors forced the people they ruled over to send their own relatives to this city. There the Aztec priests killed them to please their gods. For this cruelty the Aztecs were hated.

Aztec calendar.

Cities in the Clouds: The Incas

Long ago in South America, other Indian cities grew. These were the cities of the Incas. They were near the Pacific Ocean by the Andes Mountains in the northern part of South America. The Incas ruled over people who probably started out fishing and farming by the ocean. Later, they moved up into the mountains, probably when they found gold and silver there. The Incas decorated everything, even walls, with gold and silver!

The Big Surprise

It may seem strange to you, but for thousands of years only a few ships from Europe had "bumped into" North or South America. The few that had done so were forgotten. So when Christopher Columbus set sail from Europe, he thought his ships would go straight to Asia. He also thought it would be a short trip. He didn't even know that the huge Pacific Ocean existed. It was a big surprise when he bumped into land near North and South America.

Columbus lands in the Americas.

Here is Columbus explaining the plans for his voyage to Queen Isabella and King Ferdinand.

This is the way it happened. Queen Isabella and King Ferdinand of Spain had given Columbus ships and sailors to go to Asia, which they called the "Indies." The King and Queen weren't interested in finding new continents. They wanted to get pepper and spices from Asia that they could sell in Europe. They hoped to make a lot of money. They also wanted to spread their religion.

Do you think it's strange that Columbus and the King and Queen would go to all that trouble just for pepper? Well, they didn't have refrigerators to keep their meat from spoiling. Their dinners didn't taste very good at all! They believed the pepper would keep the meat fresher, and the spices would cover up other bad tastes. They didn't know how to grow their own pepper.

Columbus Finds a New World

Columbus and his men set sail for Asia. They sailed and sailed for two months, so long they thought they were lost. They had only three little ships: the *Niña,* the *Pinta,* and the *Santa Maria.* The sailors were just about to make Columbus turn back when they saw an island. They thought this was near the "Indies." That's why they gave the natives of America the wrong name. They called them "Indians." Descendants of these natives of America still call themselves Indians, but they are also called Native Americans. You'll hear both names in this book.

Columbus and his men had come upon a New World. That was in the year 1492. You will always remember that if you learn this rhyme:

Dover Publications (31 East Second Street, Mineola, New York 11501) has an easy-to-make Columbus Panorama and a forty-eight-page Columbus coloring book.

In fourteen hundred and ninety-two,
Columbus sailed the ocean blue

Horses and Guns

After Columbus claimed the new lands for Spain, many Spaniards came to North and South America. They battled and defeated the Indians they met. Are you surprised that small bands of Spanish soldiers could win battles over much larger numbers of Indian warriors? They won because their weapons were much stronger than those of the Indians.

The Spanish soldiers had swords, guns, and cannons. The Indians had only spears and arrows. The Spanish wore armor, which is a helmet and coat made of steel. Do you think that would protect them from spears and arrows? The Indians probably had wood and leather shields. Would that protect them from Spanish weapons?

The Spanish soldiers rode horses, too. The Indians had never seen a horse before. They thought the horse and the rider were one animal. Think how frightening that would be!

Smallpox

But something even more important worked against the Indians. They caught a disease from the Spanish. The Indians had never been exposed to the diseases of the Old World. When they got smallpox, millions of Indians died before they had the chance to fight the Spanish.

Cortés.

Cortés: The Aztecs Lose

Hernando Cortés and six hundred Spanish soldiers captured the Aztec capital and all its gold. (Earlier, Cortés had burned his ships so that his men couldn't run away!) Were these all the men Cortés had? No! Other Indians helped him. They were the people the Aztecs had ruled cruelly. It is sad to say that the Spanish didn't treat their Indian helpers much better.

And Cortés was helped by the diseases his men brought with them. These struck down the Aztecs. The Indians had actually won their first battle with the Spanish, but then they began to die by the thousands of diseases. Starvation also killed many of the Indians. Within ten years, 7 million natives would be dead.

Pizarro: The Incas Lose

Francisco Pizarro had fewer soldiers than Cortés to attack the Incas and take their treasures. It helped, though, that the Incas were arguing among themselves over who should be king.

Smallpox helped Pizarro, too. It had arrived with other new diseases before him. Again, millions died. Because so many Incas died of smallpox before even fighting against Pizarro and the Spanish, one missionary said that just the look and smell of a Spaniard caused the Indians to "give up the ghost."

The people who survived were no better off being ruled by the Spanish than being ruled by the Incas. The Spaniards forced many Indians to work in the new silver mines that were found. They were driven to work as hard as slaves.

The U.S.A.: Good-for-Nothing Lands

Many Spaniards were thrilled to hear about the incredible treasure of the Aztecs and Incas. They traveled northward from the Aztec capital in Mexico, imagining they would find more cities of gold. That was how they came to the lands that became our country. They saw the Mississippi River and the wilderness to the east and west. But they found no more empires to conquer, no more gold or silver. They called the country "good-for-nothing lands," and most went back to Mexico to settle.

Good Lands

Indians in the lands that became the United States knew that the land was good for many things. The land provided them with what they needed for food and shelter. Some Indians grew corn. Others fished or gathered nuts and berries in the woods. The women did much of the farming and provided a lot of the food. The men also worked hard and spent a lot of time hunting.

The American Indians were careful only to kill as many animals as they needed. They believed the forests should be left as they were. Unlike the Europeans, they did not think the land was "good for nothing" just because they found no silver or gold. The American Indians knew that the land they were living on was good, and so they were good to the land.

England Enters

Over one hundred years after Columbus, the Europeans who first settled our country came from England. England is an island country in the northern Atlantic Ocean. Find England on a globe. With your finger, trace a route across the Atlantic Ocean to the eastern coast of North America.

For a long time, England had been fighting Spain. English ships would try to capture Spanish ships coming from America, carrying silver and gold taken from the Aztecs and Incas.

England saw that Spain was going to own a big part of the rich "New World." The men who worked for the Queen of England wanted some of the treasure of America for themselves.

This is a map of the early colonies. You can trace and then color this map.

An Englishman named Sir Walter Raleigh set out to start a colony in North America. (A colony is an area ruled by the government of a faraway country.) Several of Sir Walter Raleigh's ships struggled across the ocean to an island off present-day North Carolina. But the English people that Raleigh sent over didn't bother to plant corn. Instead they dug for gold, which they didn't find. To get food, they had to depend on trading for it with the Indians. What is trading? Have you ever traded for something?

Does it seem like a very good idea to quarrel with people who are giving you food? NO! But the English bragged about their cities and their religion because they thought they were so much better than the Indians. The Indians refused to give them any more food. So the English had to go home.

The Lost Colony

Raleigh sailed again with more settlers, and this time the people stayed in his colony. The first baby of English parents in the New World was born there, and she was named Virginia Dare.

No one knows what happened to the little girl, though. When a ship came back from England four years after she had been born, no one was left in the village. There was no sign of what happened to Virginia Dare except an Indian word carved on a doorpost. Since everybody in the colony had disappeared, it was called "the lost colony."

Jamestown and the People of Pocahontas

Look at the map on page 121 and find the area that is now the state of Virginia. Here, in 1607, the English set up their first successful settlement at a place they called Jamestown. It was named after the English king at the time, James I.

The settlers did not know that they had picked a dangerous place for their village. The ground was swampy, and there were many mosquitoes that carried a disease called malaria. About 100 settlers had come to Jamestown, but by Christmas of the first year of the settlement, only 32 remained alive.

The Jamestown settlers had a strict leader named Captain John Smith. He helped the settlers get through some very hard times in their first years. He made them give up looking for gold and instead begin planting corn.

Still, there was not enough food at first. To get food the settlers sometimes took it from the Indians who lived in the area. Sometimes John Smith was able to trade with the Indians: he traded copper kettles and tools in exchange for corn.

The most powerful Indian leader in the area was named Wahunsonacock. He had brought together 30 Algonquin tribes under his leadership. Because he lived in a village called Powhatan, the English settlers called him Powhatan (which is still the name you are likely to see used in most books).

Sometimes the settlers and Indians fought fiercely. But, because they each had things the other wanted, they also tried to get along. John Smith said that Wahunsonacock once asked him, "Why should you take by force from us that which you can obtain by love?"

But once, John Smith was captured by the people of Wahunsonacock. Nobody knows for sure exactly what happened next. Probably Smith was soon set free. But Smith himself told another story. Years after the event, he wrote that he was about to be killed by the Indians. One young Indian girl begged that Smith's life be spared, but no one would listen. Heavy clubs were about to come down on Smith's head. Then, suddenly, the young girl rushed forward and took Smith's head in her arms. According to the story Smith told, the girl who rescued him was Pocahontas, the daughter of Wahunsonacock.

Most likely John Smith made up this story. The story has been told over and over again. It became so popular in England that people wrote poems and plays about it! Why do you think the story became so popular?

When Pocahontas grew up, she married one of the Jamestown colonists, an Englishman named John Rolfe. She traveled with her husband to England, where people thought of her as "an Indian princess."

Here is Pocahontas dressed in English-style clothes.

To learn more about life in the colonies, you can look for these books:

Colonial Life *by Bobbie Kalman (Crabtree Publishing Co.). This is part of a series called "Historic Communities," which also includes* Colonial Crafts *and* A Colonial Town.

Jamestown: The Beginning *by Elizabeth A. Campbell (Little, Brown & Co.).*

Sara Morton's Day *by Kate Waters (Scholastic). A picture book about a day in the life of a girl in colonial Jamestown.*

Pilgrims

Jamestown was the first important English settlement in our country. But soon an important English settlement was started in the north, near where Boston is today. It was started by the Pilgrims. Who were the Pilgrims?

Wild turkey.

The Pilgrims were very religious people. They came to our country to worship in a way that was not allowed in England.

The English Pilgrims stepped off their ship, the *Mayflower*, in 1620. They, too, were saved from starving by friendly Indians. When we celebrate Thanksgiving Day, we are remembering a special feast the Pilgrims held. They wanted to thank God for the food the Indians showed them how to plant and hunt. Can you think of an American bird you eat at holidays? This was a strange creature to the Pilgrims! Can you trace a drawing of a turkey or a pumpkin to color?

The Puritans

Other English colonists followed the Pilgrims to New England. These people were called Puritans. Like the Pilgrims, they were a deeply religious group of Christians, but they did not agree with the beliefs of the Pilgrims.

The Puritans settled in the area around what is now the city of Boston, Massachusetts. (Of course there was no city back then!) The Puritans believed in working hard, and their colony grew quickly. It was called the Massachusetts Bay Colony.

Puritan parents were often strict with their children. They expected the children to behave properly at all times. They also placed a great value on learning to read, because they felt it was very important to be able to read the Bible.

Puritan children would often learn their letters from books called primers. One commonly used primer, *The New England Primer*, taught a little rhyme to

Puritans at work.

go along with each letter of the alphabet. Often the rhymes had a religious meaning or tried to teach a lesson. For example, for the letter F, children read

> The idle Fool
> Is whipped at school.

You wouldn't want to be caught daydreaming in a Puritan school!

Thirteen Colonies

Over the next century (one hundred years), more and more people moved to America from Europe. Not just from England, either. New colonies were begun by different religious groups, by friends of the English king, or by business companies. After a time there were thirteen colonies in the Eastern part of the country near the Atlantic Ocean. These are now called the thirteen original colonies. Later they would become the first states of the United States.

A Trail Blazer

Can you imagine what blazing a trail could mean? Well, you may know that a trail is a path through the wilderness. Blazing a trail means marking trees with paint or cuts so others can follow where you have gone. To mark the trail, you have to cut your way through a forest thick with trees and bushes and briers. It's hard work!

More and more colonists were willing to go west from the ocean to find land to farm. Of course, they also had to face Indian attack, but first they needed someone like Daniel Boone to blaze a trail for them.

Boone crossed the mountains in what is now western Virginia and North Carolina and found land good for farming. But he was attacked by Indians. They didn't want settlers scaring off the animals they hunted. Boone stayed anyway.

A little later Boone went back across the mountains and tried several times to lead settlers west. He finally succeeded. The new log fort they built was called Boonesboro after him.

Daniel Boone.

Slavery

One large group of people who came to America didn't want to. They liked their lives in Africa, where they had their own fields and animals, governments and religion, and beautiful artisanship. They were forced to come and were made slaves, people without rights.

Crop failures and wars in Africa drove some people from their homes. Some of these people were captured and sold, mainly to English or New England ship captains. Many died on the terrible voyage across the Atlantic

Ocean. This voyage was called "the middle passage." African slaves were brought to many parts of America. They were forced to forget their country, and the governments and religions they had known there.

Most African slaves in our country were sold to owners of large tobacco, rice, or cotton farms in the South, called plantations. This kind of farm needed large numbers of workers. Some of the black people had been farmers in their own country, but many had worked as miners, or potters, or healers, or teachers. As slaves, most of them were made to work in the fields, at least at first, and the work was very hard. Some of them tried to rebel. They didn't know when they could be free, but they tried to keep their hopes alive.

The King's Mistake

Most of the colonists were demanding more land. For over a hundred years they had kept moving westward. They wanted to keep going farther. They had already fought the French and Indians for that land, but now the English King said the Indians should have it.

The King made other rules that the colonists didn't like. That was a big mistake; he was too far away in England to know what should be done. The colonists got so tired of the King's rules, they decided they should make their own laws.

Boston Tea Party.

A Tea Party

The different colonies had one argument after another with the King. Finally, a group in Boston got very angry. They dressed up as Mohawk Indians and boarded a ship in Boston harbor. Then they dumped all the tea the King wanted them to buy into the water! So you see, nobody drank tea at the Boston Tea Party!

A Famous Man

Benjamin Franklin did not like the Boston Tea Party. He hoped the King would try harder to understand what the colonists wanted. But the King was stubborn, and Franklin gave up hoping. He became a leader in the Revolution.

Benjamin Franklin.

Franklin was famous even in Europe for his inventions. He started out a poor boy, worked hard, and became successful. Americans liked to think everyone could work hard and become successful in the new country.

Ben Franklin wrote a book that gave hints about how to do well in life. One of his secrets was: "Early to bed, early to rise, makes a man healthy, wealthy, and wise."

What do you think Franklin meant? Did you ever hear anyone say: the early bird gets the worm? You know we don't really want a worm for breakfast!

A COLONIAL TREAT

We call the time when our country was made up of colonies the colonial days. Ben Franklin would have liked this healthful snack from the colonial days.

Be sure a grown-up helps you. It takes: 2 tablespoons cinnamon, ½ cup sugar, ¼ teaspoon nutmeg, 1 egg white, 1 cup nuts. (Pecans and walnuts were especially popular nuts in the colonies.)

Preheat the oven to 300°. Grease a cookie sheet. Mix cinnamon, sugar and nutmeg, in a little bowl. Put the egg white in another small bowl. (It's great fun to separate the white from the yolk!) Beat the egg white lightly and stir in the nuts, a few at a time. Make sure they're well covered.

Next, put the nuts in the spice mixture, and coat them well again. Place them on the greased cookie sheet and bake 30 minutes until crisp. Let them cool slightly on the cookie sheet. Eat warm or cooled.

A Shot Heard Round the World

All of the colonies were beginning to distrust the King. Virginia and Massachusetts were the leaders against him. In Massachusetts they even formed bands of men to be ready to go to war. They were called "Minutemen" because they could be ready to fight in a minute. They also gathered weapons at Concord, Massachusetts.

The colonists thought the British would try to take these weapons away. They had spies watching to see which way the British soldiers would come. One colonist, a patriot named Paul Revere, had arranged a signal to help him warn the others. It was: "One if by land, and two if by sea." One lamp would tell Revere that the soldiers were marching by land from Boston to Concord. Two lamps meant the British were coming by boat.

One spring night Revere saw two lamps in the window of the church tower. He knew the British would come by sea.

Paul Revere.

Suppose you were with Paul Revere that night in Boston. He jumps on his horse and pulls you up behind him. You gallop through the night over the rough road. The wind is in your face, and you are cold.

Suddenly Paul Revere shouts out loud, and you forget you are uncomfortable in the excitement. He is calling: "The Redcoats are coming! The Redcoats are coming!" You see people throwing open their doors and lighting lanterns. The Minutemen are getting ready.

The next day you are at Lexington. So are the Minutemen and the British, who wear red coats. They face one another. Shots are fired. The American Revolution has begun.

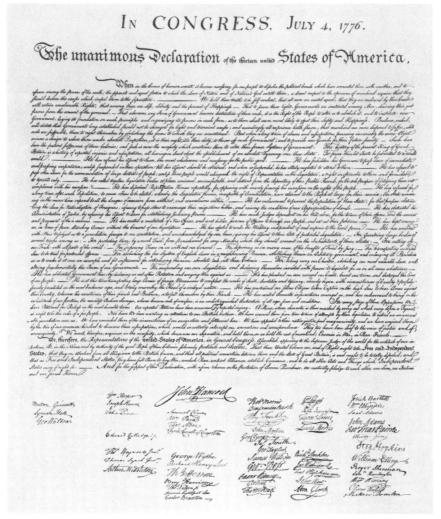

The Declaration of Independence.

Thomas Jefferson.

Birthday

In 1776, a year after the fighting started, the colonists decided to begin a new country, the United States. This is what we celebrate on July 4, the signing of the Declaration of Independence. This is our country's birthday.

Thomas Jefferson wrote the Declaration of Independence. It declared that all men are created equal.

No one had ever started a country before with that idea. Jefferson was one of our greatest countrymen. He was also our third president.

The Liberty Bell.

Liberty Bell

The Liberty Bell rang out the news of independence. Why would the colonists need a bell to tell them news? Did they have radio, television, or telephones?

The people of Philadelphia needed the bell to tell them to gather together for the first reading of the Declaration of Independence.

After independence was won, the Liberty Bell was rung on special occasions. Almost sixty years later, it cracked. But it remains a symbol of our country. You can still see the Liberty Bell if you go to Philadelphia.

Do you have a small bell in your home to ring? There are still bells in church towers. You can draw a bell and color it.

Freedom for All?

Did the Declaration of Independence make women as free as men? Did it free all the slaves? No. People don't change all at once. The men who signed the Declaration couldn't have agreed on these questions. The only African slaves who could be free were the few who joined the Army or were freed by their owners.

Two Women

Abigail Adams.

Abigail Adams was the wife of one of the most important men behind the Revolution. His name was John Adams and he helped to write the Declaration. She scolded him for not asking women to agree to the new laws. She said the women would not obey them!

A young woman named Deborah Sampson wanted to join the Revolutionary Army. She pretended to be a young man by wearing men's clothes. Then she joined the Army! She fought bravely until she got sick. A doctor found out her secret, so she left the Army.

Two Freed Women

Two slave women actually won their freedom. Elizabeth Freeman told a judge in Massachusetts that the new law of the state made her free. Judges are people who help decide what the laws mean. The judge agreed with her, so she became a free woman.

Phillis Wheatley was born in Africa and sold as a slave to John Wheatley of Boston. He gave her his name. She wanted to learn to write English, and the Wheatley family taught her. She wrote poems so well

Elizabeth "Mumbet" Freeman.

they were printed in a book. The Wheatleys freed her, and she married. She kept writing. She even sent a letter to George Washington.

Do you know a poem? Have you ever tried to write a poem as Phillis Wheatley did? You probably could!

A Father

George Washington was the man who did the most to win the War of Independence. He led the Army that fought the British and won. You can imagine how hard it was for a poor, new country to buy guns and horses and even boots for soldiers. There were times when Washington's men walked in the snow without warm coats and shoes!

After the war, Washington helped to build a strong government. He became the first President because everyone trusted him. Even though he would have preferred to be at his home, Mount Vernon, with his wife, Martha, he agreed to become President and was in office for eight years. This is why he is called the Father of His Country. The new capital city of the country was named "Washington" to honor him. Can you find it on your map?

George Washington leading his troops.

A Cherry Tree

There is a legend about George Washington as a boy. We are not sure the story is true, but it shows how honest everyone believed Washington to be.

Young George was given a new hatchet. He tried it out by cutting down one of his father's favorite cherry trees! Naturally his father was angry. He asked George: "Who cut down the tree?"

George knew he could be punished. There were other people he could have tried to blame it on. But he said: "Father, I cannot tell a lie. I cut down your cherry tree with my new hatchet."

Twice as Big

Have you ever heard your parents or your friends say: "I got a bargain"? You probably know they meant that they bought something for a lot less money than it was worth.

Our third President, Thomas Jefferson, bought for our country probably the greatest bargain that ever was. He wanted to buy one small but important city. This was New Orleans, on the Mississippi River.

Instead, France wanted to sell everything she owned west of the thirteen states, including the little city of New Orleans. The price was so low and the land so huge, Jefferson said *Yes*!

Overnight our country was more than twice as big. Just look at the map where it says Louisiana Purchase.

President Jefferson sent Lewis and Clark and nearly fifty other men to explore the new land. He wanted to know what rivers and plants and animals were there.

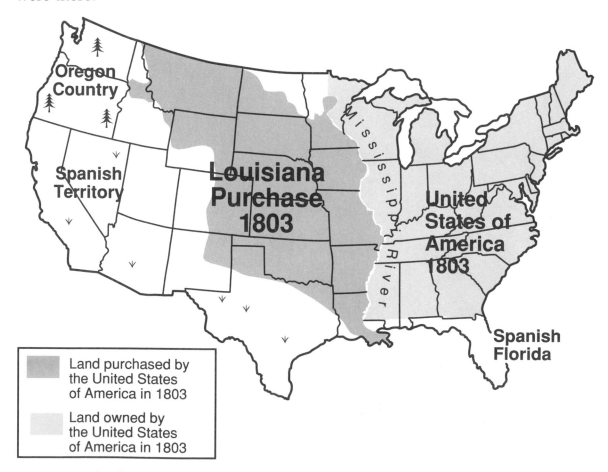

Oregon Country

Spanish Territory

Louisiana Purchase 1803

Mississippi River

United States of America 1803

Spanish Florida

Land purchased by the United States of America in 1803

Land owned by the United States of America in 1803

With a lot of help from an Indian woman named Sacajawea, the explorers went all the way to the Pacific Ocean. They came back with reports of furs and friendly Indians. Traders and trappers rushed to find these furs.

Lewis and Clark talk with Indians they meet on their travels.

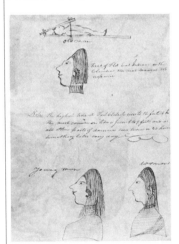

Here are some of Clarke's drawings, pictures of Chinook Indians.

As Lewis and Clark traveled, Clark kept notes and drew pictures about what they saw in a journal. Next time you travel, you can keep a journal about what you do and see by collecting pictures. Or, you can keep a picture journal right now, like this. For a week sit down every day and draw or cut out pictures of things you've seen or things you like. For this project you will need pencil, paper, scissors, tape or glue, and some old magazines or newspapers.

Dover Publications (31 East Second Street, Mineolia, New York 11501) has a forty-five-page Lewis and Clark Expedition coloring book.

The Fight Goes On

The Indians on the land roamed freely, hunting buffalo and other animals. The European settlers wanted to stay in one place on the land, so they could farm. They fought the Indians for new land when they had to. The Indians fought back. Both sides were hurt, and began to hate one another. The Indians were forced to move again and again. Some struck back fiercely and made the settlers hate them even more.

Sequoyah

One of the Indian tribes called the Cherokee had a written language. This happened because an Indian named Sequoyah invented eighty-five symbols to stand for the sounds of the Cherokee language. They were later to write a sad story. The Cherokee were forced to leave their homes and move hundreds of miles west along a "Trail of Tears."

Sequoyah with his alphabet.

What's Left?

West of the Louisiana Purchase, where California and the other Western states are now, the land was owned by Spain. In the early times of our country, the Spanish kept this land. But not many Spanish settlers went north from Mexico into this huge territory. Yet Spain still said it was hers.

In the early days, Spain also kept Florida. There, on the northeastern shore, they started a city even before the English settled at Jamestown. It is called St. Augustine, and it is still there. Not many Spanish lived in Florida in the early days. But Indians went there. Many traveled to Florida from the United States to escape the European settlers.

Will the settlers want to move into Florida? Will there be more wars with the Indians there? Will the settlers want to move into the Spanish lands out in the far west? These are stories you will hear later, but for now you can see the Spanish lands on the map of the Louisiana Purchase.

III.

FINE ARTS

Introduction
to the Fine Arts

FOR PARENTS AND TEACHERS

A child needs to observe and make art in order to understand and appreciate the arts. A book alone cannot adequately convey the experience of music or the impact of visual art. This book *can* hope to provide basic knowledge about art, but parents, teachers, and children themselves must play the main role. Nothing can replace visiting galleries, attending performances, listening to recordings, and encouraging children to sing, paint, sculpt, and play-act for themselves.

Although the place of the fine arts in a child's early education is a subject filled with uncertainties and intangibles, civilizations since the time of the Greeks, and possibly before then, have understood that artistic education can have an ennobling effect upon children.

The arts are rightly stressed in many of our elementary schools. Experiences of poetry, music, dance, architecture, and visual arts not only bring joy to children, but also stir and energize their minds with examples of beauty and accomplishment. The development of their artistic sensibilities can enhance the development of their moral sensibilities. It is well understood that stories of good and great actions help instill ideals and values in children. Similar benefits come from children's experience of high achievements in painting, dance, architecture, and sculpture. Today, most schools in the civilized world act upon this principle in their educational policies.

But finally, the value of art in our lives is not just its utility in instilling high ideals in children. Making and appreciating art introduces them to a realm of delight that can last all their lives. Their experiences of the arts can make their lives happier than they would otherwise be.

The Fine Arts

In this section, we are going to learn some things about the fine arts of music, painting, dance, sculpture, and architecture. We will explain what they are, but to get a good idea of them, you have to experience them for yourself.

Did you know that you have already done some of them? When you paint a picture you are doing art. When you make up stories you are doing literature. When you sing, you are making music. When you move to music, you are dancing. When you play house with dolls, or pretend to stop a runaway train, you are doing drama. If you build a snowman or a clay shape, you are doing sculpture. And when you build castles in the sand you are making architecture.

Literature

Literature is mainly stories and poems. We won't say more about the art of literature here, because there is a whole section of this book that is devoted to stories and poems.

Music

Piano.

Music is an art that just about everyone loves. It is made up of sounds that go together. Music is what people sing, and play on instruments like the piano. In fact, one of the best ways to learn about music is to sing, so let's start off by singing songs. Two of the most famous children's songs are "Row, Row, Row Your Boat," and "London Bridge Is Falling Down." Let's sing them.

Row, Row, Row Your Boat

Row, row, row your boat
Gently down the stream,
Merrily, merrily, merrily, merrily,
Life is but a dream.

London Bridge Is Falling Down

London Bridge is falling down,
Falling down, falling down,
London Bridge is falling down,
My fair lady!

You will find music everywhere, if you listen for it. Of course, you find it playing on the radio and on the stereo or tape player. But music is also used for parades, weddings, dances, and on the football field when the band plays at half-time. You find music in churches and temples and other holy places. Soldiers used to go to war marching to music!

This is because music can express how we feel, sometimes even better than words can. A big band playing "The Star-Spangled Banner" can make you feel proud, a fast song can make you want to dance, and a sad song can even make

you want to cry. The next time you watch a movie, listen for the music in the background. Close your eyes and listen hard. You will be amazed how much music you hear that you didn't even notice before. It can make a sad part seem even sadder, or a scary part seem even scarier.

Different pieces of music can give us very different feelings. Let's sing four very different songs, and see how you feel when you are singing each of them.

Yankee Doodle

Yankee Doodle went to town,
Riding on a pony,
He stuck a feather in his cap,
And called it Macaroni.

How did you feel when you sang that? Did you feel like clapping your hands and marching around? Most people do.

Hush, Little Baby

Hush, little baby, don't say a word,
Papa's going to buy you a mockingbird.
And if that mockingbird don't sing,
Papa's going to buy you a diamond ring.

How do you feel singing that song? All quiet and warm? Even a bit sleepy? Don't you feel quite different from the first song?

Here We Go Round the Mulberry Bush

Here we go round the mulberry bush,
The mulberry bush, the mulberry bush,
Here we go round the mulberry bush,
So early in the morning.

Doesn't it make you want to dance and move? And now let's sing "The Star-Spangled Banner."

The Star-Spangled Banner

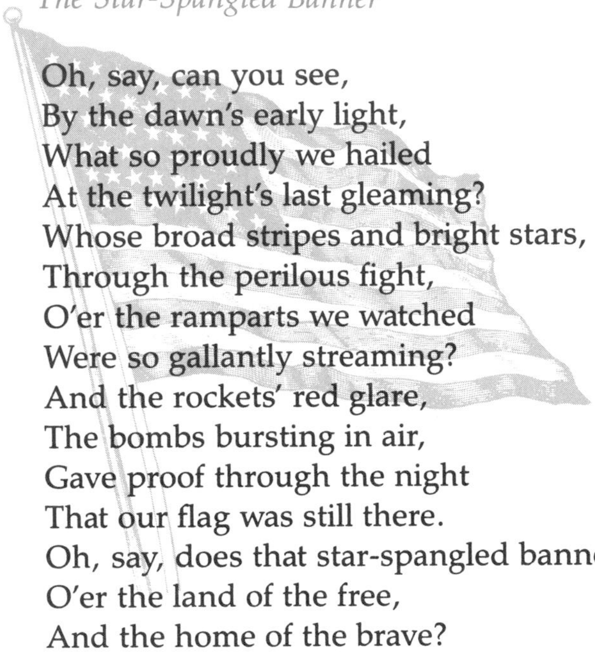

Oh, say, can you see,
By the dawn's early light,
What so proudly we hailed
At the twilight's last gleaming?
Whose broad stripes and bright stars,
Through the perilous fight,
O'er the ramparts we watched
Were so gallantly streaming?
And the rockets' red glare,
The bombs bursting in air,
Gave proof through the night
That our flag was still there.
Oh, say, does that star-spangled banner yet wave
O'er the land of the free,
And the home of the brave?

How does that make you feel? Proud, as if you want to stand up as straight as you can?

You see, music can make you feel many different things, sometimes even in the same song.

Vocal and Instrumental Music

Songs are called vocal music because you use your voice to sing them. (The word vocal comes from an old word for "voice.") The music you play on an instrument like the piano is called instrumental music.

Two of the most popular musical instruments are the piano and the guitar. Can you think of some other musical instruments?

The Many Different Kinds of Music

People around the world love to sing and play music, and every country has its own kind. Here in the United States, where we have many different kinds of people, we have many different kinds of music. Folk music, classical music, jazz music, religious music, country music, rock-and-roll music, and popular music are just some of the kinds of music we have here in America. Can you think of some others? We will learn about many different kinds of music as we go along.

Folk Music

Folk music is one of our oldest forms of music. In fact, many of the songs that you probably already know are folk songs. Let's sing one:

Down in the Valley

Down in the valley, the valley so low,
Hang your head over, hear the wind blow.
Hear the wind blow, dear, hear the wind blow,
Hang your head over, hear the wind blow.

Writing this letter, containing three lines,
Answer my question, will you be mine?
Will you be mine, dear, will you be mine?
Answer my question, will you be mine?

Roses love sunshine, violets love dew,
Angels in heaven, know I love you.
Know I love you, dear, know I love you.
Angels in heaven, know I love you.

Folk songs have been passed down from parents to their children (and their grandchildren, and so on) for many years. Folk songs are often about many of the things we do every day, such as working and playing and traveling. They help make doing these things more enjoyable.

Imagine working on the railroad, with trains going by, and whistles blowing as you sing the next song. Notice how you speed up when you sing "Dinah, won't you blow your horn!" just like a train going faster and faster. In this way the song imitates the trains you are singing about, and makes you feel as if you're right on the train.

I've Been Working on the Railroad

I've been working on the railroad,
All the live long day.
I've been working on the railroad,
Just to pass the time away.
Can't you hear the whistle blowin'?
Rise up so early in the morn',
Can't you hear the captain shoutin',
"Dinah, blow your horn!"
Dinah, won't you blow?
Dinah, won't you blow?
Dinah, won't you blow your horn?
Dinah, won't you blow?
Dinah, won't you blow?
Dinah, won't you blow your horn?

Classical Music

People who write music are called composers. One of the greatest composers of all time was named Wolfgang Amadeus Mozart. That's a lot to say, so most people just call him Mozart.

Mozart lived in Europe over two hundred years ago, just about the time our country began. Mozart started playing and writing music when he was very, very young. In fact, he composed music on the piano when he was only five years old! One of the songs that

Mozart.

Aaron Copland conducts an orchestra.

Mozart loved to play is a song we still sing today: "Twinkle, Twinkle, Little Star." Let's sing it now.

Twinkle, Twinkle, Little Star

Twinkle, twinkle, little star,
How I wonder what you are.
Up above the world so high
Like a diamond in the sky.
Twinkle, twinkle, little star,
How I wonder what you are!

Young Mozart rehearsing.

One reason that Mozart was so good at music was that his father's job was teaching music, so you might say that music was in Mozart's family. He had a sister called Nannerl, who played the violin while Mozart played the piano. They played so well together that kings and queens and princes used to ask to hear them perform. As children, they traveled with their father to many different cities and countries in Europe, playing before kings and queens and large crowds of people.

Mozart wrote what we call classical music. One kind of classical music he wrote is called a symphony. A symphony is a long piece of music, played by a large group of musicians called an orchestra.

Mozart is also famous for his operas. An opera is a kind of play where people sing instead of talk. One of Mozart's operas is called *The Magic Flute*. It's about a flute that makes such beautiful music it can work magic on those who hear it. Many feel that Mozart's music is like that—it is so beautiful that it works magic.

Jazz

Jazz is a kind of music that was born in America. It comes from the chants and rhythms that black people brought from Africa and mixed with the music that they found here.

Jazz was born in New Orleans, which is in the southern part of the United States, near the mouth of the Mississippi River. One of the most popular songs in New Orleans, even today, is one of the favorite songs of jazz: "When the Saints Go Marching In." Let's sing it now.

When the Saints Go Marching In

I am just a weary pilgrim,
Plodding through this world of sin,
Getting ready for that city,
When the Saints go marching in.

Oh, when the Saints go marching in,
When the Saints go marching in,
Oh, I want to be in that number,
When the Saints go marching in.

Can you feel how you want to clap and stamp your feet when you sing this song? Much of jazz, especially the first kind of jazz—which is called Dixieland Jazz—has this exciting, bouncy quality.

Louis Armstrong.

LOUIS ARMSTRONG

One of the people who made jazz famous was a man named Louis Armstrong. His friends called him "Satchmo." When he was a boy, he was very poor, and he used to sing in the streets of New Orleans. He would follow behind the brass bands that marched there, learning the songs they played. Later, he learned to play a cornet, which is a kind of horn made of brass. On the riverboats that went up and down the Mississippi River he played and sang a new sort of music called jazz. When he moved north to Chicago on Lake Michigan, he found that the people in Chicago loved jazz just the way they did in New Orleans. "Satchmo" became so famous that he played his music all across America. He played so well that the others in the band would stop playing, or play very quietly, just to listen to him alone. This is called playing a solo (solo means alone), and he was the first to play solos in jazz.

He had such a warm smile that people enjoyed just watching him sing and play. He became very famous, and appeared in movies and on television. He went around the world playing jazz, and made friends for America and its music everywhere.

The Three Parts of Music: Melody, Rhythm, and Harmony

Now we are going to tell you about how music works. There are three parts to music: melody, rhythm, and harmony. When you listen to a song on the radio or stereo, you can usually hear all three parts of music.

First, you hear someone singing. That is the melody.

Then, if you listen hard, you will hear drums pounding away. That is the rhythm.

And finally, you will hear instruments playing in the background. They are playing chords which form the harmony.

Let's learn a little more about each of these parts of music.

Melody

When you sing a song, the part that you are singing is called the melody. The melody is the tune that you sing the words to.

What makes a good melody? Why do you like to sing some songs better than others? That is one of the things people have been trying to figure out for a long time. It's like trying to say what makes a good story. You can tell when you've heard one, just the way you can tell when you've heard a good melody.

Here are two very different American songs that have melodies people admire.

Oh, Susanna!

I come from Alabama with my banjo on my knee.
I'm going to Louisiana,
My Susanna for to see.
Oh, Susanna!
Don't you cry for me,
For I come from Alabama with my banjo on my knee.

America the Beautiful

Oh, beautiful for spacious skies,
For amber waves of grain;

For purple mountain majesties,
Above the fruited plain.
America!
America!
God shed His grace on thee,
And crown thy good with brotherhood,
From sea to shining sea.

What you were just singing was the melody. It is the main part of a song.

Rhythm

Rhythm is what you play on drums, or clap with your hands, or tap with your toes, while a song is playing. To show you what we mean, let's now play the game, "Pat-a-cake, Pat-a-cake." Sit opposite a friend, and clap when your parent or teacher shows you, if you haven't learned this game. You clap your own hands or your friend's, on the words we have underlined.

Pat-a-Cake

Pat-a-cake, pat-a-cake, baker's man.
Bake me a cake, as fast as you can.

Now clap the whole song!

Pat-a-Cake

Pat-a-cake, pat-a-cake, baker's man!
Bake me a cake as fast as you can.
Pat it and prick it and mark it with a "B,"
And put it in the oven for baby and me.

When you were clapping, you were clapping out the rhythm of the song.
When people skip rope, they often say a rhyme like "Pat-a-Cake" and clap. It tells you when to skip. The rhythm to a song is like that. It tells you when to sing.
You can clap or snap your fingers or play drums to any song, if you want

to. All music has rhythm. In fact, there are some kinds of music that are mainly rhythm. The music of the tribes of some Native Americans, and some tribes in Africa, is made up mainly of rhythm.

The next time you run very fast, when you come to a stop, put your hand over your heart. Can you hear your heart beating? Even you have a rhythm.

Harmony

Harmony is the hardest part of music to explain. Harmony is a way of making different notes sound good when they are sung together or played at the same time. When someone sings the melody and someone else sings or plays notes in the background, that is harmony.

The next time you listen to a song on the radio or stereo, try to pick out the three parts of music. First, you hear someone singing—that is the melody. Then, if you listen for them, you will usually hear drums pounding away. That is the rhythm. And you will hear the instruments (like the piano and guitar) playing in the background. They are playing the chords that form the harmony. These three things, melody, rhythm, and harmony, are the three parts of music.

Dance

When you hear music, do you ever feel like tapping your toes, or clapping your hands, or marching around? As long as people have heard music, it seems, they have wanted to move to it. And they have wanted to move in a way that looked good.

That is what dance is. Dance is moving your body in time to music, to rhythm. There are many different kinds of dances. People have used dance for many different things. Some people dance to thank heaven for lots of food. Some people dance to pray for rain. Some people dance to tell a story. People dance in order to meet each other, as a way of saying hi! People dance just to say they are happy. Maybe you have danced just because you felt like it.

Folk Dancing

Folk dancing is done to folk music. There are different kinds of folk dances, and most of them go back many years.

One of the most popular kinds of folk dancing in the United States is called square dancing. People dance in squares (which is why it's called square dancing), in circles, and straight lines. A "caller" tells them where and how to move. And all the time they keep moving, forming different shapes and patterns. Sometimes they move in a circle one way, and then the other, sometimes they weave around each other as though they are tying a knot together. And in a way they are. Because dancing can bind people together, and can make you feel close to other people.

Ballet

Ballet is a way of telling a story by dancing. It is performed on a stage in front of an audience. Ballet is often danced to classical music that is played by an orchestra. The orchestra sits in the pit, a low space in front of the stage.

Male ballet dancers are known for the great leaps and spins they can make. Female ballet dancers often wear special slippers that help them dance on tiptoes and twirl with ease. It takes many years of hard work to dance this way, and many ballet dancers start when they are your age or younger. They must do difficult exercises to make their muscles strong and flexible like rubber bands. Then they can jump so high, they look like they are flying!

Ballerina.

Tap Dancing

Have you ever heard a song and just started tapping your toes? People liked to tap their toes so much that a whole kind of dancing came from it, called tap dancing.

Tap dancing came from a mixture of dancing from different places including Africa. People used to put coins on their shoes so they could make the clicking sound when they danced. They liked to hear the different rhythms they could make with their feet.

Art

Art Is Found in All Times and Places

Art is another word for painting, drawing, and sculpture. Art goes back all the way to the Stone Age, when people lived in caves! That is over twenty thousand years ago—a hundred times as old as the United States is!

Look at these pictures of animals that were painted in caves in France. Do you recognize the horse in the picture? Can you draw a picture of a horse? As you are drawing, notice how the artists back then drew theirs.

Cave painting.

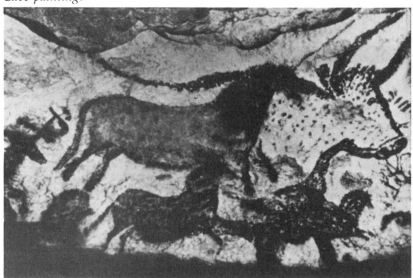

Parents and teachers: Using a large cardboard box for a cave, children can make their own cave art.

You can also find cave art in the United States. Native Americans painted and carved pictures of people and animals on cave walls and cliffs in almost every state in this country.

Symmetry and Patterns in Arts and Crafts

Some art that is very, very old comes from Egypt, which is in northern Africa. Here is a picture of a small sculpture—actually used for a headrest!—from ancient Egypt. Can you see how one side of the headrest is like the other side? You could say the two sides mirror each other. In art, when two sides mirror each other, it is called symmetry. Let's look more closely. See how there is a lion on each side looking away from the god Shu in the middle? And do you see that one side of the god's body is the same as the other side? Both arms are raised the same way. Both legs are folded under his body. What else is the same on both sides? We find symmetry in many arts and crafts around the world.

Egyptian headrest.

Along with symmetry we also often find repeating patterns. Look at the way the two lions are identical. They repeat the same shape. Even the four lines on their sides are repeated. What other patterns repeat in the headrest?

Native Americans use symmetry and repeating patterns when making pottery, rugs, and blankets. See how the diamond design of this Navajo rug repeats over and over? See how the two sides of the rug are symmetrical? Next look at the water jug made by the Zuni

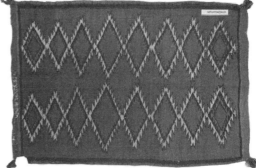

Navajo rug.

Zuñi Indian water jar.

Shaker drawing: The Tree of Life.

Indians. It uses a repeating pattern of animal shapes, but it does not use symmetry.

You can also find repeating patterns and symmetry in the art of other people around the world. You can see them in the folk art of the Shakers of New England and in rich, colorful oriental rugs.

You can make a symmetrical picture. Fold a piece of paper in half. Then unfold it and draw or paint a design on one side of the fold. Then mirror your design on the other side of the page. Does your picture use repeated patterns and symmetry?

Here's a way you can make a picture with repeating patterns that is also symmetrical. The steps in the picture will help you. (Step 1) Take a square sheet of paper. (Step 2) Fold it in half, first up and down, (Step 3) then sideways, (Steps 4 and 5) and finally along both diagonals. (Step 6) Now fold all the corners into the center exactly. (Step 7) Unfold the paper. Trace over your folds with colored crayons.

Now draw patterns in the spaces on both the left and right side of your sheet, as we've done. Try different patterns, or color in different areas. Doesn't it look great?

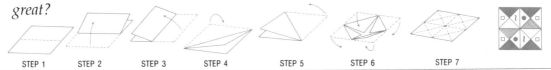

STEP 1   STEP 2   STEP 3   STEP 4   STEP 5   STEP 6   STEP 7

Portraits

Pictures of people are called portraits. In the old days painters would make portraits of people just the way we take photos of our friends today. Portraits tell us a lot about the people in them. The people can seem happy or sad, ugly or beautiful, or even cruel or kind. When you look at portraits, try to see what the artists are saying about the people in them.

Here are two famous portraits. An American named James Whistler painted this picture of his mother. See how he painted her whole body? Some portraits are like that. What do you think Whistler's mother would be like if you met her?

Whistler's picture of his mother.

The painting in the picture on this page is called the *Mona Lisa*. The *Mona Lisa* was painted by an Italian painter named Leonardo da Vinci. See how da Vinci painted *Mona Lisa*'s head and only part of her body? This is another way to do a portrait. What is she thinking about with that strange smile of hers? Is she happy or sad? Can you tell?

Would you like to draw or paint a portrait? You could make a portrait of a friend, a member of your family, or someone in your class at school. You could even make a portrait of yourself, which is called a "self-portrait." Are you going to show the whole body or just the head and part of the body?

Leonardo da Vinci's Mona Lisa.

Architecture and Sculpture

Architecture is a big word. It can mean the art of design of buildings—buildings like your school, your church or temple, your library, even your house or apartment building. Tall buildings like the Empire State Building, big buildings like palaces and castles and city hall are part of architecture. The igloos that Eskimos build out of ice and the teepees of American Indians, as well as grass huts and log cabins, are all kinds of architecture.

Igloo.

Some of the oldest buildings in the world are the pyramids in Egypt. A pyramid was a tomb, or a burial room, for the king of Egypt. Pyramids were filled with secrets and treasure! Pyramids are very, very large—many times bigger than a house—and made out of heavy stones.

You might like to build a pyramid out of clay. To make a pyramid, first draw a square on a piece of paper. Make the clay fit inside the square. Now pile on clay higher and higher, but make it come to a point at the top.

Would you like to make a statue of the Sphinx to go beside your pyramid? A Sphinx is a strange beast that has the head of a person and the body of a lion. It's pretty hard to make that out of clay, but you might want to try.

Sphinx.

The Statue of Liberty.

Sculpture is another word for statues—statues of people or lions or horses, for example—like those you see in the park, or at museums, or in front of buildings. Near the real pyramids, in Egypt, there is a statue of a Sphinx.

Can you guess what is the most famous statue in America? It's the Statue of Liberty. The Statue of Liberty was given to America by France, because our country stands for liberty.

There are many statues in America, but none quite like the Statue of Liberty. It's so big, you can walk around inside. It stands at the entrance to New York Harbor with its torch raised, and it tells people coming in on ships that liberty in our country is like a torch that shines in the dark.

IV.
MATHEMATICS

Introduction to Mathematics—Grades One Through Six

Americans do not pay enough attention to mathematics in the early grades. As a proportion of total class time, we spend less time on mathematics and more time on language arts than other countries do. Yet those other countries outshine us not only in math, but also in language arts. Their children's reading and writing levels are as high as or higher than ours by seventh grade. Do they know something we don't know? Yes, and we must change our ways.

It is almost impossible for children *not* to practice the use of language. Their out-of-school practice in speaking and listening helps their performance in reading and writing, since there's a lot of overlap between listening, talking, reading, and writing. But, with so little time spent on math, it is all too easy for children to neglect practicing mathematics, which is a kind of language. Just as English should become second nature to our children, so should math.

The three cardinal principles of early mathematics education are 1) practice, 2) practice, and 3) practice. Not mindless, repetitive practice, but thoughtful and varied practice. We know that these three principles are true, because they hold for learning in *all* subjects. Well-meaning persons who are concerned to protect the joy of the childhood years wrongly fear that applying these three principles to mathematics portends a soul-killing approach to schooling.

Nothing could be further from the truth. What destroys joy in mathematics is not practice but anxiety—anxiety that one is mathematically stupid, that one does not have that special numerical talent. But math talent is no more rare than language talent. The number of great mathematicians and the number of great poets per million of population are roughly similar. Yet people experience math anxiety to a much greater degree than language anxiety, because their early training has denied them systematic familiarity with the vocabulary, grammar, and spelling of mathematics. Those of us who experience math anxiety must resolve not to inflict this educational wound upon our children.

The basic operations of math must be familiar before the principles behind those operations are well understood. Again, an analogy with language learning is pertinent. Most people agree that it's important to learn the alphabet at an early age, before one understands the full significance of the alphabet. (A deep understanding of the alphabet is confined to professors of linguistics.) Being instantaneously familiar with the sums and differences of any two digits is even more basic than knowing the alphabet. Such knowledge is on a par with knowing basic sentences of English—which is a stage prior to knowing the alphabet.

While practice is the watchword of math, intelligent, fun practice is the hallmark of good math teaching. One teaching hint is worth remembering at all levels of math. Children should be encouraged to practice the same operation or types of problems from several different angles. This is a highly useful way to begin to grasp the relationships behind math operations.

Since intelligent practice and problem-solving activities are essential to learning math, it is very **important to note that the math section of this book must be regarded as a supplement, not as a sufficient vehicle for teaching mathematics.** The section is, in effect, a detailed *summary* of the math that should be mastered in this grade. We have thought it important to include these summaries to help parents and teachers ascertain that children have in fact learned the math they should know in each grade. The math sections must be used in conjunction with imaginative problems and activities taken from workbooks, from standard math texts, or from the imaginations of teachers and parents.

Familiarity-through-practice in the early grades is a sure road to making mathematics fun, and it's the only road to conquering fear and anxiety in mathematics. Those who follow this very basic teaching principle in early grades will win the gratitude of their children in later years.

Introduction to First-Grade Mathematics

During first grade, it is important for students to acquire a solid base for their future work in mathematics, particularly in three areas: addition, subtraction, and place value. Students should learn the addition and subtraction facts up to 12 very well, and also learn to work with them in various ways. For instance, they should be able to name all the addition facts that have the same sum, or answer problems like $9 - \underline{} = 5$ comfortably. Students should also get their first practice at mental arithmetic, learning to solve problems like $43 + 5 = 48$ in their heads.

In working with place value, students need to acquire a good understanding of the difference between tens and ones. For instance, they should be able to divide any 2-digit number into tens and ones, or compare 2-digit numbers using the signs $>$, $<$, and $=$.

Students are also introduced to geometry, fractions, word problems, and money during first grade. In each of these areas, they should have a good knowledge of the material presented in this section by the end of the year.

It is particularly important that the more challenging sorts of questions in this section be a regular part of the curriculum for all students. In U.S. textbooks, these types of questions are often omitted, or put in as extra practice for students who are ahead of the class. In countries that are more successful at teaching mathematics than we are in this country, these kinds of questions are a regular part of the practice for all students throughout first grade. In answering such questions, students must understand the mathematics involved securely and use it flexibly. Thus students in these countries generally have a much more secure foundation than U.S. students, both in remembering what they have learned and in solving new complex problems.

Students in this country deserve to have the same kind of foundation in mathematics. With consistent and regular practice, students can master the material in this section, and be well prepared for mathematics in the second grade, and beyond.

First-Grade Mathematics

Numbers from 0 to 10

Numbers from 1 to 10

Numbers tell how many *of* something there are.

There is 1 bird:

There are 2 kittens:

There are 3 boats:

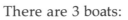

There are 4 pigs:

There are 5 green balls and 7 white ones.

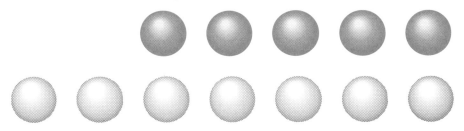

Here are the numbers from 1 to 10 in order:

1, 2, 3, 4, 5, 6, 7, 8, 9, 10.

They can also be written out in words:

one, two, three, four, five, six, seven, eight, nine, ten.

Learn to count from 1 to 10 fast without making any mistakes. Also learn to write the words for the numbers up to 10.

Putting numbers in order from smallest to largest is called ordering. For example, to order the numbers, 9, 6, 8, 7, you would write 6, 7, 8, 9. Notice that 6 comes before 7, and that 8 comes after 7.

6, 7, 8
before   after

Zero

0 is a special number. It is spelled out zero. Zero tells how many you have when you don't have any. You had a pencil, but you lost it. Now you have 0 pencils.

Maria has never seen a train. She has seen zero trains.

Working with the Numbers Up to 10

In counting, the number that comes after another number is always 1 more. For example, 6 is one more than 5. If you had 5 apples and you got 1 more, you would have 6 apples.

In counting, the number that comes before another number is always 1 less. For example, 3 is 1 less than 4. If you had 4 pencils, and you gave 1 away, you would have 3 pencils left.

Notice that to figure out what is 1 less, you count backward. Learn to count backward from 10 to 0, like this:

10, 9, 8, 7, 6, 5, 4, 3, 2, 1, 0.

Addition

Addition, the + Sign and the = Sign

Addition means putting numbers together. There are 3 flowers in a glass. You pick 2 more flowers and put them in the glass also. How many flowers are in the glass?

This is an addition problem, because you start with 3 flowers and add 2 more. To figure the problem out, count how many flowers are in the glass in the second picture. There are 5 flowers in all. We write this problem: $3+2=5$. It can be written out: Three plus two equals five.

The sign $+$ means plus. It shows that you are adding.

The sign $=$ means equals. Equals means "is the same as": $3+2=5$ because $3+2$ is the same as 5. You could also say $5=5$.

Here is another addition problem. There are 3 blocks.

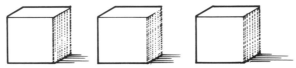

You add 4 more.

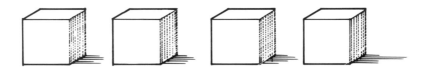

Count how many blocks there are altogether. There are 7. We write this problem: $3+4=7$.

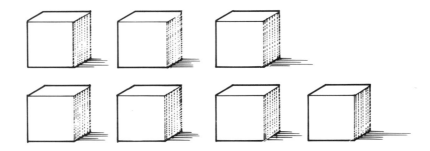

The Sum and Ways of Saying Addition

When you add two numbers together, the answer you get is called the sum. The sum of $3+2$ is 5. The sum of $3+4$ is 7.

There are different ways of saying $3+2=5$. People say "three plus two equals five," or "three plus two is five," or "three and two make five." Notice that the $+$ sign can also be read as "and," and that people sometimes say "is" or "make" for the $=$ sign.

Adding in Any Order and Adding 0

It does not matter what order you add numbers in, the sum is still the same: $3+4=7$ and $4+3=7$. This rule makes it easier to learn addition facts. If you know $6+2=8$, then you know $2+6=8$.

When you add 0 to a number, you get that number as an answer: $0+5=5$ and $7+0=7$. You can understand this because 0 means "nothing," and when you add nothing to a number you get that number. This rule makes it easier to learn addition facts with 0.

Addition Facts Up to 5

$3+2=5$ is an addition fact. Learn all the addition facts with sums from 0 to 5. Here is a list of them.

Sum of 0	Sum of 1	Sum of 2	Sum of 3	Sum of 4	Sum of 5
$0+0=0$	$1+0=1$	$2+0=2$	$3+0=3$	$4+0=4$	$5+0=5$
	$0+1=1$	$1+1=2$	$2+1=3$	$3+1=4$	$4+1=5$
		$0+2=2$	$1+2=3$	$2+2=4$	$3+2=5$
			$0+3=3$	$1+3=4$	$2+3=5$
				$0+4=4$	$1+4=5$
					$0+5=5$

Addition Facts with Sums from 6 to 8

Learn all the addition facts with sums from 6 to 8. You can see that these addition facts follow the same pattern.

Sum of 6	Sum of 7	Sum of 8
$6+0=6$	$7+0=7$	$8+0=8$
$5+1=6$	$6+1=7$	$7+1=8$
$4+2=6$	$5+2=7$	$6+2=8$
$3+3=6$	$4+3=7$	$5+3=8$
$2+4=6$	$3+4=7$	$4+4=8$
$1+5=6$	$2+5=7$	$3+5=8$
$0+6=6$	$1+6=7$	$2+6=8$
	$0+7=7$	$1+7=8$
		$0+8=8$

Practicing Addition Facts

One way to practice addition facts is with objects that you can count, like buckets. For example, to learn what 3 + 5 equals, start with 3 buckets.

Then add 5 more buckets.

Count how many buckets you have in all: 8. So 3 + 5 = 8.

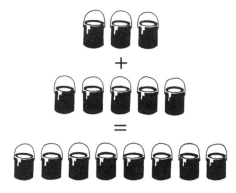

Another way to practice is to count forward. What does 5 + 2 equal? You want the number that is 2 more than 5. So count forward 2 numbers from 5, like this: 5 → 6, 7. So 5 + 2 = 7.

When you know how to find addition facts by counting, practice them until you know them by heart, without counting. Make sure to practice writing and saying the addition facts a lot. It is very important that you be able to give the sums of addition facts quickly, without making mistakes.

Addition Facts with Sums of 9 and 10

Learn all the addition facts with sums of 9 and 10. You do not need to learn 10 + 0 = 10 as a separate addition fact. If you learn how to add together the numbers from 0 to 9, you will be able to solve any addition problem.

Sum of 9	Sum of 10
9 + 0 = 9	9 + 1 = 10
8 + 1 = 9	8 + 2 = 10
7 + 2 = 9	7 + 3 = 10
6 + 3 = 9	6 + 4 = 10
5 + 4 = 9	5 + 5 = 10
4 + 5 = 9	4 + 6 = 10
3 + 6 = 9	3 + 7 = 10
2 + 7 = 9	2 + 8 = 10
1 + 8 = 9	1 + 9 = 10
0 + 9 = 9	

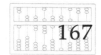
Addition Facts with the Same Sum

Learn to give all the addition facts that have the same sum. For example, if you were asked for all the addition facts with a sum of 6, you would write: $6+0=6$, $5+1=6$, $4+2=6$, $3+3=6$, $2+4=6$, $1+5=6$, $0+6=6$.

One good way to practice addition facts is with 2 sets of owls of different colors. Here is how you can show all the addition facts that have a sum of 7, using black and green owls.

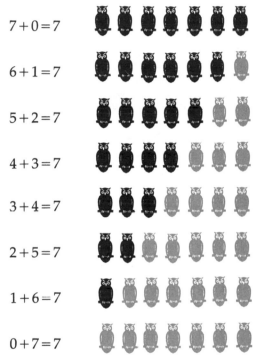

$$7+0=7$$

$$6+1=7$$

$$5+2=7$$

$$4+3=7$$

$$3+4=7$$

$$2+5=7$$

$$1+6=7$$

$$0+7=7$$

Another Way to Write Addition

There is another way to write addition. For example:

$5+3=8$ can also be written

$$\begin{array}{r} 5 \\ +3 \\ \hline 8 \end{array}$$

$2+5=7$ can also be written

$$\begin{array}{r} 2 \\ +5 \\ \hline 7 \end{array}$$

Learn to write addition in both ways.

Addition with Three Numbers

To add three numbers, add the first two numbers, and then add the third number. For example, to solve

$$4$$
$$2$$
$$+1$$

First add

$$\begin{array}{r} 4 \\ +2 \\ \hline 6 \end{array}$$

Then add the third number:

$$\begin{array}{r} 4 \\ 2 \\ +1 \end{array} \quad \begin{array}{r} \,6 \\ +1 \\ \hline 7 \end{array}$$

So

$$\begin{array}{r} 4 \\ 2 \\ +1 \\ \hline 7 \end{array}$$

Here is another example:

$$\begin{array}{r} 2 \\ 5 \\ +3 \end{array} \quad \begin{array}{r} 2 \\ 5 \\ +3 \end{array} \quad \begin{array}{r} \,7 \\ +3 \\ \hline 10 \end{array}$$

So

$$\begin{array}{r} 2 \\ 5 \\ +3 \\ \hline 10 \end{array}$$

Greater Than and Less Than

Greater Than

The number 5 is greater than the number 4, because 5 is one more than 4. For example, 5 baseball mitts are more than 4 baseball mitts.

We say 5 is greater than 4. This can also be written 5>4.

The sign > means "is greater than."

Notice that 5 also comes after 4. Numbers that are greater come after in counting.

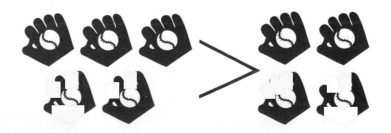

Less Than

The number 3 is less than the number 4. For example, 3 nickels are less than 4 nickels.

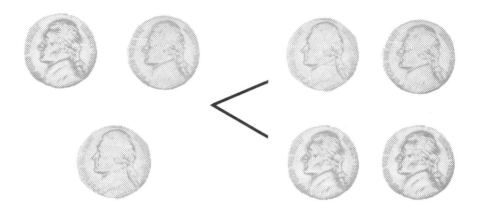

We say 3 is less than 4. This can also be written 3<4. The sign < means "is less than."

Notice that 3 comes before 4. Numbers that are less come before in counting.

Learn to compare numbers using the signs >, <, and =. Remember that the equals sign means "is the same as." Here are some examples: 10>3 6<8 9=9

Notice that the small end of the signs > and < always points to the smaller number.

Comparing Sums with >, <, and =

You can also use the signs >, <, and = to compare sums.

4+3>4+2 because 4+3=7
            4+2=6
        and 7>6

3+1=2+2 because 3+1=4
            and 2+2=4

Learn to write >, <, and = in problems like these:
4+4>7   2+5=6+1   3+6<3+7

Subtraction

Subtraction Means Taking Away

Subtraction means taking a number away. Suppose there are 5 glasses of grape juice on the table, and Pam takes 2 of the glasses away, and drinks them. How many glasses are left on the table?

Count them. There are 3 glasses left. In numbers, this is written:

$$5 - 2 = 3$$

Or it can be spelled out: Five minus two equals three.

The sign − means minus, and it shows that you are subtracting. You can also say, "Five take away two is three." Take away means the same thing as minus.

Practicing Subtraction Facts

$5 - 2 = 3$ is a **subtraction fact.** There are many subtraction facts to learn, just as in addition.

One way to practice subtraction facts is with counters, like buckets. To figure out what $7 - 3$ equals, start with 7 buckets. Then take away 3 buckets. Count how many you have left: 4. So $7 - 3 = 4$.

Another way to practice is to count backward. What does $9 - 4$ equal? You want the number that is 4 less than 9, so count backward 4 numbers from 9, like this: $9 \rightarrow 8 \rightarrow 7 \rightarrow 6 \rightarrow 5$. So $9 - 4 = 5$.

The Difference

$$7 - 3 = 4 \qquad \text{The difference is 4.}$$

The number you have left after you subtract is called the difference. So the difference of $7 - 3$ is 4. What is the difference of $4 - 3$? 1, because 4 minus 3 equals 1.

Notice that in subtraction we ask "how many are left," because we are taking a number away.

In addition we ask, "how many in all," or "how many altogether," because we are adding numbers together.

Learning Subtraction Facts Up to 10

When you know how to find subtraction facts by counting backward, learn the subtraction facts up to 10 by heart. Practice writing and saying these subtraction facts many times. You should know them so well that you don't have to stop to figure them out.

Subtraction Facts from 0, 1, 2, 3, 4, and 5

From 0	*From 1*	*From 2*	*From 3*	*From 4*	*From 5*
$0-0=0$	$1-0=1$	$2-0=2$	$3-0=3$	$4-0=4$	$5-0=5$
	$1-1=0$	$2-1=1$	$3-1=2$	$4-1=3$	$5-1=4$
		$2-2=0$	$3-2=1$	$4-2=2$	$5-2=3$
			$3-3=0$	$4-3=1$	$5-3=2$
				$4-4=0$	$5-4=1$
					$5-5=0$

Subtraction Facts from 6, 7, and 8

From 6	From 7	From 8
6−0=6	7−0=7	8−0=8
6−1=5	7−1=6	8−1=7
6−2=4	7−2=5	8−2=6
6−3=3	7−3=4	8−3=5
6−4=2	7−4=3	8−4=4
6−5=1	7−5=2	8−5=3
6−6=0	7−6=1	8−6=2
	7−7=0	8−7=1
		8−8=0

Subtraction Facts from 9 and 10

From 9	From 10
9−0=9	10−1=9
9−1=8	10−2=8
9−2=7	10−3=7
9−3=6	10−4=6
9−4=5	10−5=5
9−5=4	10−6=4
9−6=3	10−7=3
9−7=2	10−8=2
9−8=1	10−9=1
9−9=0	

Another Way to Write Subtraction

There are two ways to write subtraction, just like addition.

$$8-6=2 \text{ can be written} \quad \begin{array}{r} 8 \\ -6 \\ \hline 2 \end{array}$$

$$5-4=1 \text{ can be written} \quad \begin{array}{r} 5 \\ -4 \\ \hline 1 \end{array}$$

Learn to write subtraction in both ways.

Comparing Differences with >, <, and =

The signs >, <, and = can be used to compare differences as well as sums. Here are some examples: $10-2>6$ $\qquad$ $8-4=7-3$ $\qquad$ $6-4<5-1$

Fact Families

Fact Families Are Patterns

To help learn the subtraction facts, learn this pattern:

$$7-2=5 \text{ and } 7-5=2$$
$$6-4=2 \text{ and } 6-2=4$$
$$8-5=3 \text{ and } 8-3=5$$

This pattern is part of a fact family. Fact families relate addition facts to the subtraction facts that are their opposites. To see how this works, start with 5 soldiers. Add 2 more soldiers. This shows that $5+2=7$.

$$5+2=7$$

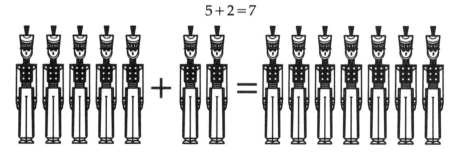

Now take away the 2 soldiers. How many do you have left? 5. This shows that $7-2=5$. So $7-2=5$ is the opposite of $5+2=7$. In $7-2=5$ you took away the 2 soldiers that you added in $5+2=7$.

$$7-2=5$$

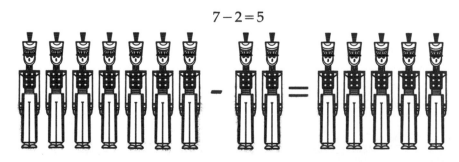

In the same way $2+5=7$ is the opposite of $7-5=2$.

$$2+5=7$$

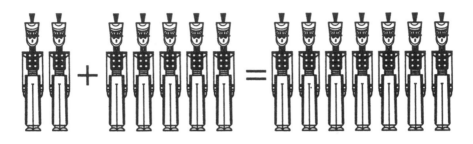

$$7-5=2$$

These four facts make a fact family:

$$5+2=7\text{-------}7-2=5$$
$$2+5=7\text{-------}7-5=2$$

Notice how the numbers at the beginning and end of the addition facts switch places to make the subtraction facts that are their opposites.

Learn to find the facts in a family. For example, if you are given $4+2=6$, find the other facts in the family. The other facts are $2+4=6$, $6-2=4$, $6-4=2$.

Ordinal Numbers

There are 10 skunks. Which one is not in line? The seventh skunk. The seventh skunk is skunk number 7. When you name the number of something in an order, you use the ordinal numbers. You can remember the name of ordinal numbers if you remember they help you put things in order. Here are the first 10 ordinal numbers:

1st   2nd   3rd   4th   5th   6th   7th   8th   9th   10th

Learn to say and write these first 10 ordinal numbers in order. Notice that except for first, second, and third, ordinal numbers end in "th."

Place Value

10 is different from the other numbers we have learned so far, because it has 2 digits. A digit is any of the single numbers from 0 to 9. 10 has 2 digits, a 1 and a 0.

The first digit is the tens' place and the second digit is the ones' place. The 1 in the tens' place means 1 group of ten.

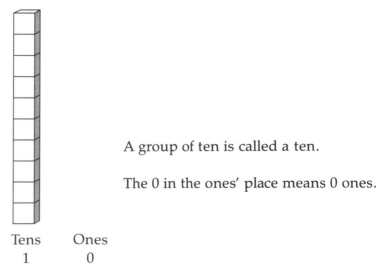

A group of ten is called a ten.

The 0 in the ones' place means 0 ones.

Tens   Ones

1   0

The next number is 11:

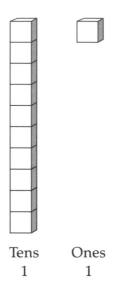

Tens   Ones
1   1

11 means 1 ten and 1 one.

The next number is 12: 1 ten and 2 ones.

The numbers continue: 13, 14, 15, 16, 17, 18, 19.

19 means 1 ten and 9 ones.
After 19, the next number is 20.

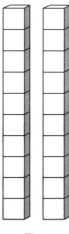

Tens   Ones

20 means 2 tens and 0 ones.

The numbers from 11 to 20 are written out: eleven, twelve, thirteen, fourteen, fifteen, sixteen, seventeen, eighteen, nineteen, twenty.

Place Value from 21 to 100

After 20, the numbers continue 21, 22, 23, 24, 25, 26, 27, 28, 29, 30. 25 means 2 tens and 5 ones.

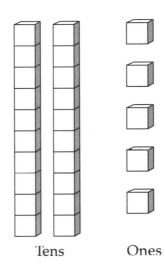

Tens   Ones

30 means 3 tens and 0 ones. 40 means 4 tens and 0 ones. Counting by tens we have:

10, 20, 30, 40, 50, 60, 70, 80, 90

These numbers are written out: ten, twenty, thirty, forty, fifty, sixty, seventy, eighty, ninety.

67 means 6 tens and 7 ones.

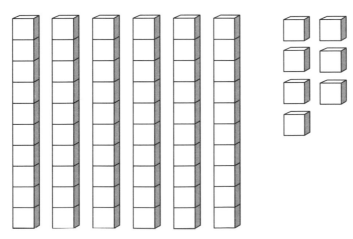

Tens   Ones

93 means 9 tens and 3 ones.

The numbers continue to 99—9 tens and 9 ones. After 99, the next number is 100. 100 is spelled out one hundred.

Working with 2-Digit Numbers

Learn to name the number that comes before and after a 2-digit number. For example, 46 comes before 47. 48 comes after 47. Also learn to name the number that is one more and one less. One more than 52 is 53. One less than 60 is 59.

Also learn to compare 2-digit numbers using the signs >, <, and =. When you compare 2-digit numbers, always look at the tens' place first. When a 2-digit number is greater in the tens' place, it must be greater. For example, 73>67. Here are two more examples: 39<56   43=43

Counting to 100

Practice counting out loud from 1 to 100, so that you can do it easily.

Practice counting to 100 by tens: 10, 20, 30, 40, 50, and so on. Practice counting to 100 by fives: 5, 10, 15, 20, 25, 30, and so on.

You should also be able to count by tens, starting on different numbers, like 14: 14, 24, 34, 44, 54, 64, 74, and so on. Notice that when you count by tens, the ones' place stays the same, but the tens' place gets 1 number larger each time.

Also practice counting backward from one ten to another. For example, count backward from 30 to 20 like this: 30, 29, 28, 27, 26, 25, 24, 23, 22, 21, 20.

You should be able to name any number between 0 and 100. For example, 78 is "seventy-eight."

You should be able to read any number between 0 and 100 when it is spelled out. For example, eighty-three is 83.

Arithmetic and Calculators

Math that has to do with numbers and counting and adding and subtracting is called arithmetic. All the math we have done so far has been arithmetic.

People often use a calculator to do arithmetic—after they have learned their addition and subtraction facts by heart! A calculator can add and subtract numbers. It can also do many other things with numbers. It looks like this:

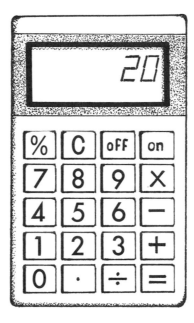

Geometry

Geometry and Flat Shapes

Math that has to do with shapes (both flat shapes and solid shapes) is called geometry.

Learn to recognize the following flat shapes.

A triangle. A triangle has three sides.

A rectangle. A rectangle has four sides.

A square. A square has four sides of equal length.

A circle.

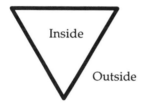

Each of these shapes has an inside and an outside.

The circle is inside the triangle. The square is outside the triangle.

Geometry and Solid Shapes

Learn to recognize these solid shapes.

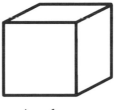

A cube.

A sphere.

Also learn the difference between open figures and closed figures:

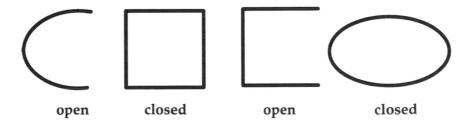

open   closed   open   closed

Fractions

A fraction is a part of something.

½ is a fraction. If something is divided into 2 equal parts, each part is ½. ½ is written out one half.

Each part is ½ of the circle.

⅓ is also a fraction. If something is divided into 3 equal parts, each part is ⅓. ⅓ is written out one third.

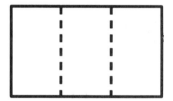

Each part is ⅓ of the rectangle.

If something is divided into 4 equal parts, each part is ¼. ¼ is written out one fourth. It is also sometimes called one quarter.

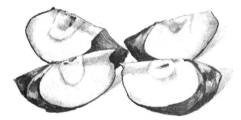

Each part is ¼ of the apple.

Not all parts are equal. Equal parts are the same size. For example, the parts of the square on the next page are not equal. The parts of the rectangle are equal.

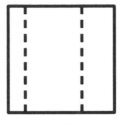

| The square has 3 parts. | The rectangle has 4 parts. |
| The parts are not equal. | The parts are equal. |

Learn to recognize the fractions ½, ⅓, and ¼. For example, the shaded part of the circle is ⅓. The shaded part of the cube is ¼.

   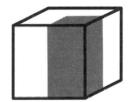

The shaded part is ⅓.   **The shaded part is ¼.**

Telling Time

You can use the numbers you have learned so far to tell time. A clock or a watch has a short hand for the hours, and a longer hand for the minutes.

When the minute hand (the long hand) is on the 12, and the hour hand (the short hand) is on the 8, then it is 8 o'clock: 8 o'clock is sometimes written 8:00. It means 8 hours and no minutes.

8:00 or 8 o'clock.

When the minute hand is on the 12, and the hour hand is on the 4, then it is 4 o'clock. Learn to write either 4 o'clock or 4:00.

Time before noon is called A.M. A.M. is in the morning. Time after noon is called P.M. P.M. is in the afternoon, or at night. So 8 A.M. is 8 o'clock in the morning, and 8 P.M. is 8 o'clock at night. Learn to say whether a time is A.M. or P.M. For example, 4 o'clock in the afternoon is 4 P.M.

4:00 P.M.

Whenever the minute hand is on the 12, look at the hour hand. The number that the hour hand is on tells you what "o'clock" it is. It is 10 o'clock on the clock pictured here.

10:00 or 10 o'clock.

When the minute hand is on the 6, and the hour hand is between the 7 and the 8, it is 7:30: 7:30 is spelled out seven-thirty.

7:30 or seven-thirty.

The "thirty" stands for 30 minutes: 7:30 means 7 hours and 30 minutes. 30 minutes is ½ of an hour. A whole hour is 60 minutes. 60 minutes is the time that it takes for the minute hand to go all the way around the clock, starting at the 12 and coming back to the 12. In that time the hour hand moves from one number to the next number. 1 hour has passed.

Whenever the minute hand is on the 6, it shows that there are 30 minutes. It is 2:30.

2:30 or two-thirty.

Digital clocks do not have hands. On them the time appears in numbers. So 8 o'clock would look like this,   and 7:30 would look like this.

The Calendar

There are 7 days in a week: Sunday, Monday, Tuesday, Wednesday, Thursday, Friday, Saturday.

This is a calendar.

You should be able to say the names of the days out loud in order.

There are 12 months in the year: 1) January, 2) February, 3) March, 4) April, 5) May, 6) June, 7) July, 8) August, 9) September, 10) October, 11) November, 12) December.

You should be able to say the names of the months out loud in order.

Do you remember ordinal numbers, the ones that help you put things in order? You can learn two new ordinal numbers to go with the last two months of the year: eleventh and twelfth. November is the eleventh month, and December is the twelfth month.

H*ere's a rhyme for the months that you can learn by heart:*

> ## THIRTY DAYS HATH SEPTEMBER
> *Thirty days hath September,*
> *April, June, and November;*
> *All the rest have thirty-one,*
> *Excepting February alone.*
> *And that has twenty-eight days clear,*
> *And twenty-nine in each leap year.*

More Addition and Subtraction

Addition and Subtraction Facts to 12

By the end of the first grade, you should know all the addition and subtraction facts up to 12 by heart.

Here are all the addition facts with sums of 11 and 12. Notice that none of the numbers that are added together is more than 9. That is because, if you know how to add together the numbers between 0 and 9, you can do any addition problem.

Sum of 11	*Sum of 12*
9 + 2 = 11	9 + 3 = 12
8 + 3 = 11	8 + 4 = 12
7 + 4 = 11	7 + 5 = 12
6 + 5 = 11	6 + 6 = 12
5 + 6 = 11	5 + 7 = 12
4 + 7 = 11	4 + 8 = 12
3 + 8 = 11	3 + 9 = 12
2 + 9 = 11	

Here are all the subtraction facts that begin with 11 and 12. Notice that none of the subtraction facts has a difference of more than 9. That is because each subtraction fact is the opposite of an addition fact. If you know all the subtraction facts, you can do any subtraction problem.

From 11	From 12
11−2=9	12−3=9
11−3=8	12−4=8
11−4=7	12−5=7
11−5=6	12−6=6
11−6=5	12−7=5
11−7=4	12−8=4
11−8=3	12−9=3
11−9=2	

Practice these new addition and subtraction facts until you have learned them by heart also. Because these new facts use larger numbers, they need even more practice.

More Addition and Subtraction:

There is another way to ask addition and subtraction facts:

$$7 + \underline{} = 9$$

In words, this says:

Seven plus what equals nine?

$7+2=9$. So the answer is 2.

Here is another example. $\underline{} - 3 = 9$. $\underline{12} - 3 = 9$.

Practice all the addition and subtraction facts you have learned in this way. When you can do problems like these easily, you know your addition and subtraction facts very well.

2-Digit Addition

You can use the addition facts you have learned so far to do addition with numbers that have 2 digits.

For example, to add

$$\begin{array}{r} 43 \\ +25 \\ \hline \end{array}$$

first add the 3 and the 5 in the ones' place:

tens ones

↓ ↓

$$\begin{array}{r} 4\ 3 \\ +2\ 5 \\ \hline 8 \end{array}$$

then add the 4 and the 2 in the tens' place:

tens ones

↓ ↓

$$\begin{array}{r} 4\ 3 \\ +2\ 5 \\ \hline 6\ 8 \end{array}$$

So the answer is 68. Altogether you have 6 tens and 8 ones.

Sometimes one of the numbers you are adding has two digits, but the other has only one digit. For example, find the sum.

$$\begin{array}{r} 22 \\ +\ 6 \\ \hline \end{array}$$

This kind of problem is solved in the same way. First, add the numbers in the ones' place. Then, since there are no tens to add to the 2 in the tens' place, you bring it down into the answer.

$$\begin{array}{r} 2\ 2 \\ +\ \ 6 \\ \hline 8 \end{array} \qquad \begin{array}{r} 2\ 2 \\ +\ \ 6 \\ \hline 2\ 8 \end{array}$$

The sum is 28, or 2 tens and 8 ones. Do not forget the 2 tens in your answer!

Here is a problem like this. Because it works the same way you do not need to learn it as a separate addition fact.

$$\begin{array}{r} 10 \\ +\ 2 \\ \hline 12 \end{array}$$

2-Digit Subtraction

In the same way, you can use the subtraction facts you have learned to do subtraction with 2-digit numbers.

Find the difference.

$$
\begin{array}{r}
7\ 6 \\
-3\ \ 4 \\
\hline
\end{array}
$$

First subtract in the ones' place:

$$
\begin{array}{cc}
\text{tens} & \text{ones} \\
\downarrow & \downarrow \\
7 & 6 \\
-3 & 4 \\
\hline
 & 2
\end{array}
$$

Then subtract in the tens' place:

$$
\begin{array}{cc}
\text{tens} & \text{ones} \\
\downarrow & \downarrow \\
7 & 6 \\
-3 & 4 \\
\hline
4 & 2
\end{array}
$$

So the difference is 42, or 4 tens and 2 ones.

Here is another example.

Solve:

$$
\begin{array}{r}
5\ 7 \\
-\ \ 6 \\
\hline
\end{array}
\qquad
\begin{array}{r}
5\ 7 \\
-\ \ 6 \\
\hline
5\ 1
\end{array}
$$

The answer is 51, or 5 tens and 1 one.

Practice doing many 2-digit addition and subtraction problems.

Working with Tens

The numbers 10, 20, 30, 40, 50, 60, 70, 80, 90 have the same relationship to each other as the numbers 1, 2, 3, 4, 5, 6, 7, 8, 9. For example, $2+3=5$ and $20+30=50$. $5-4=1$ and $50-40=10$. Learn how to add and subtract tens quickly in this way. By remembering that $5+2=7$, you should know right away that $50+20=70$.

The number before 3 is 2, and the ten before 30 is 20. The number after 5 is 6, and the ten after 50 is 60. Learn to work with the tens in this way. For example, the ten after 70 is 80.

Mental Addition and Subtraction

Practice adding and subtracting in your head. You know how to solve

$$\begin{array}{r} 4\,0 \\ +\ \ 7 \\ \hline 4\,7 \end{array}$$

When problems like this are simple, learn to solve them in your head. Here are some examples.

$$10+3=13 \qquad 50+5=55$$
$$14+4=18 \qquad 19-3=16$$

Also learn to add 3 numbers in your head. First add the first 2 numbers. Then add the third number.

$$7+3+5=\underline{} \qquad 8+4+4=\underline{}$$
$$10\ +5=15 \qquad 12\ +4=16$$

Counting Money

Penny   *Nickel*   *Dime*   *Quarter*

A penny is worth 1¢.
   The sign ¢ means cent.
   A nickel is worth 5¢.
   A dime is worth 10¢.
   A quarter is worth 25¢.
   Learn the names of each of these coins and how much they are worth. Money can be helpful in practicing counting, adding, and subtracting.

How much money is pictured?
Count by tens for the dimes: 10¢, 20¢, 30¢
Count by fives for the nickels: 35¢, 40¢, 45¢
Count by ones for the pennies: 46¢, 47¢, 48¢
So 48¢ is pictured.

If you start with a quarter, counting 10¢ for each dime looks a little different:
1 quarter: 25¢   3 dimes: 35¢, 45¢, 55¢   3 pennies: 56¢, 57¢, 58¢   There is 58¢ in all.

Remember that when you count by tens, the ones' place stays the same, but the tens' place gets 1 number larger each time.

Same Amount

Learn to make the same amount using different coins. For example, a nickel is worth 5¢, and 5 pennies are worth 5¢. So 5 pennies are worth the same as 1 nickel. 2 nickels are worth 10¢. So 2 nickels are worth the same as 1 dime. A quarter is worth 25¢. Learn three different ways to make the same amount as 1 quarter. To make 25¢ with nickels, count by five for each nickel: 5¢, 10¢, 15¢, 20¢, 25¢: 5 nickels make 25¢. 2 dimes and a nickel also make 25¢. So do 1 dime and 3 nickels. Practice counting out all three ways of making the same amount as 1 quarter.

Word Problems with Money

Learn to solve word problems with money.

Susan buys a container of milk for 55¢ and an apple for 32¢. How much money does she spend in all?

This is an addition problem. To solve it, add

$$\begin{array}{r} 55¢ \\ + \ 32¢ \\ \hline 87¢ \end{array}$$

You get 87¢. So Susan spends 87¢ in all.

Chris has 75¢, but he spends a quarter on a video game. How much does he have left?

This is a subtraction problem. To solve it, you first have to remember that a quarter is 25¢. So you have to subtract 25¢ from the money that Chris had:

$$\begin{array}{r} 75¢ \\ - \ 25¢ \\ \hline 50¢ \end{array}$$

Chris has 50¢ left.

Math Stories

Practice making up your own addition and subtraction stories. Then write down the problem you have made up in numbers and solve it. Here is one example. Kim has 12 sections of orange. She eats 7. How many sections of orange does Kim have left? You would write down: $12 - 7 = 5$. Kim has 5 pieces of orange left.

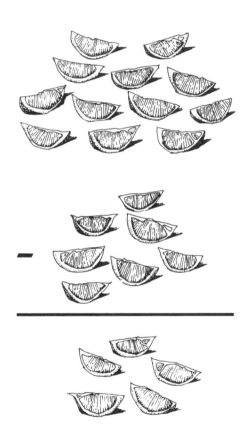

V.

NATURAL SCIENCES

Introduction to Life Sciences

A child's chief knowledge of the natural world must be gained by direct experience, not from books. To understand the plant and animal worlds, a child must observe plants and animals, preferably in natural settings, and, second-best, in museums and school laboratories. But book-learning does have tremendous importance in bringing system and coherence to a young child's knowledge of nature. Only through systematic presentation of topics can a child make steady and secure progress in scientific learning. The child's development of scientific knowledge and understanding is in some ways a very disorderly and complex process, different for each child. But a systematic approach to the topics of life science can at least provide essential building blocks for deeper understanding at a later time. Such a systematic approach ensures that huge gaps in knowledge, like ignorance of the function of flowers, will not hinder later understanding.

This first book presents an overview of the basic classes of things in nature: animal, plant, mineral, the differences between evergreen and deciduous plants, the relation of flowers to seeds, and the use of seeds as human and animal food. It differentiates between plant- and flesh-eating animals, and describes the different habitats of plants and animals. It discusses dinosaurs and pets. Finally it presents basic topics in human health: some organs of the body, the senses, some diseases, drugs, and poison.

In making this selection of topics for beginning life science, our committees were guided both by their wide experience in teaching young children and by the careful sequences that have been developed in nations that have had outstanding results in teaching elementary science: Sweden, West Germany, France, and Japan. In addition, our committee members consulted reports by the American Association for the Advancement of Science, and had discussions with the staff of the National Science

Foundation. There is no one best sequence for the systematic development of scientific knowledge, but we are certain that the one chosen is a good one that has proved itself to be effective.

That said, I must repeat: no sequence can be truly effective without direct, hands-on experience of and observation of the natural world, plus imaginative help from parents and teachers in stimulating the child's natural curiosity and interest in the natural world.

Life Sciences

PLANTS AND ANIMALS

People have said that there are three main kinds of things in the world—plants, animals, and minerals. Plants and animals are living things, but minerals are nonliving things. Sand is a mineral. Grass is a plant. Birds and people are animals.

The World of Plants

Can you imagine a world without plants? No trees to sit under during the hot summer, no grass to sit on, no peas or potatoes to eat. Plants give us and other animals food, water, and shelter. We would not be here if it were not for plants.

Many plants grow from seeds. Some seeds are so small you can hardly see them. Others are as big as a coconut. Seeds contain tiny beginnings of the plant—the roots, the stem, and the leaves—plus food to help these parts develop. You can think of it this way: a seed is a little plant in a box with its lunch, and will grow if the conditions are right.

Let's pretend you are a tree, to see how a plant works. Pretend you are standing on the soil or dirt. Does the tree stand on the top of the soil like a block on a tabletop? No. If it did, the wind would blow it over. What does the tree send into the soil to help it stand up? Roots. Roots are very strong, and they help keep the plant in the soil. But roots also help to feed the plant, by taking in nutrients and water from the soil. Nutrients are chemicals that help the plant make food.

If your feet and legs are your roots, what comes next? The trunk. Point to *your* trunk. On smaller plants, this part is called a stem. Little stems are bendable, but big tree trunks are woody and hard to bend. Stems hold the plant up and send food and water back and forth to the different parts of the plant.

Look at the tree again, and raise your arms up into the air. Up, up, all the way up! Spread your fingers as far as they will go. What does the tree have that looks like your arms and fingers, reaching toward the sky?

Your arms are like branches, and your fingers are like twigs. In the winter, you can see these branches and twigs easily on many trees. (You can put your arms down now.)

Why do you think the tree spreads its branches and twigs toward the sky? So the *leaves* can soak up the sun and breathe in the air. The leaves take in sunlight and air, and with the water and nutrients from the roots the leaves make food for the plant.

Deciduous and Evergreen Plants

In many parts of our country some trees and bushes lose their leaves in the fall. Because the leaves *fall* off at that time, we call that time of year "fall." The trees whose leaves drop are called "deciduous," a word that means "falling off." Deciduous plants get rid of their leaves before the cold weather starts, so they won't have to work too hard in winter making food.

But some trees stay green in winter. These are called evergreens, because they stay green "forever," or at least until they die. Some evergreens like pines have special leaves called needles, which are narrow and covered with wax to protect them in cold weather, just as lip wax can protect your lips in winter.

This pine tree is an evergreen.

Flowers and Seeds

Many plants make flowers. If everything goes just right, these flowers make seeds, and the seeds make new plants. If the seeds drop into the soil, and if they get enough water and nutrients, they will develop into new little plants.

  Remember this? "a seed is a little plant in a box with its lunch." That's why many animals eat seeds for food; they are packed with food that helps living things grow. Have you seen a bird eat seeds? Did you know that we humans eat seeds all the time? Yes! Nuts are seeds. Rice

is a seed. And wheat seeds are ground up to make flour, which we use to make bread, cakes, and cookies.

Animals

A fish is an animal. So is a ladybug. A tiger is an animal. So is a lizard. Animals are living things just like plants, but are different in two main ways: 1) most plants make their own food, but animals can't; and 2) most animals move themselves around, but plants can't. Although animals can't make their own food, they *can* travel around looking for it.

Some animals eat only plants, others eat only animals, including insects, and some eat both plants and animals.

Plant-eating animals come in all shapes and sizes. The elephant has developed a long trunk, which helps it reach way up into the trees! Cows have developed special, four-part stomachs that help them digest the plants they eat.

Most flesh-eating animals must be very fast to catch their dinner. Lions and tigers run very fast. Others are very sly, and hide patiently until they can pounce on their prey. Mountain lions hide high up in the rocks, and jump down on their meals.

Many insect-eating animals fly. You can see why if you think about it. Some birds catch insects right in the air, and that's not an easy thing to do.

Some animals will eat both plants and animals. Bears are animals that eat plants, flesh, and insects. They eat berries, and they eat small animals like fish, too. They also like to rip open logs with their sharp claws and eat the insects they find.

This lioness has caught a gazelle.

This brown bear pulled a salmon right out of the stream.

What about you? You are an animal; what do you like to eat? Do you eat plants and animals? You probably don't eat insects, but some people in the world do. They eat ants and grasshoppers, believe it or not!

The Food Chain

Living things have to eat to live. Plants take nutrients and water from the soil, breathe air, and use sunlight. But animals must eat living things, including plants and animals. Little creatures are eaten by bigger ones, but when big animals die, they may be eaten by smaller ones. All this eating is called "the food chain." Here's how it works.

Here's how a simple food chain works.

A bear dies and falls on the soil. Its body rots away, putting nutrients into the soil. A plant grows in the soil using the nutrients that came from the bear. An insect eats the leaves of the plant. A fish eats the insect. A bear eats the fish. The bear dies of old age, rots away, and becomes part of the soil. A plant grows from the soil, and the process starts again.

Habitats

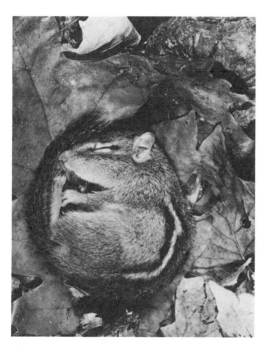

What is this chipmunk doing?

A habitat is the place where a plant or animal lives. You can think of a habitat as an animal's or plant's address—where it spends most of its time. Plant and animal habitats can be found everywhere—in the air and high in the treetops, in the forest, in meadows and prairies, in fresh water or salt water, in deserts, and even underground.

Most animals and plants have adapted to their habitats. In order to live there, they develop special ways to take in food, air, and water, and special places to make their homes and escape their enemies. In this part we will describe some habitats and the creatures who live there.

Air and Treetop Habitats

Animals that have wings often have habitats in the air and the treetops. Birds spend much of their time in the air in search of food and water, and often build their nests in trees. Bees fly in search of flowers to bring food back to their hives, which they sometimes build in trees.

Bald eagle chicks in their treetop nest

Forest Habitats

This raccoon is looking for food.

Another kind of habitat is the forest. Different kinds of forests support different animals and plants. For example, squirrels are attracted to oak forests. Can you guess why? Because squirrels like to eat acorns, which are the seeds of oak trees. Raccoons can be found in many types of forests because raccoons eat many different things.

Many animals live on the forest floor, because it is easy to find food here. When leaves fall, they start to pile up. Snails and other animals eat the leaves, and raccoons and other animals eat the snails. Does this sound familiar? It is part of the food chain!

Meadow and Prairie Habitats

Other creatures live in the meadows, among plants like grass that like lots of sunlight. Wildflowers grow very well in meadows, and sometimes create a carpet of color from one end of a meadow to the other. Very, very big meadows are called prairies. Can you think of some animals that live in meadows or prairies? How about prairie dogs? Prairie dogs are not dogs at all but squirrel-like animals with short tails. They eat lots of grass.

Water Habitats

Some animals and plants live in ponds, lakes, and rivers, and some live in the ocean. Fish live in lakes, ponds, and rivers, and eat smaller fish, plants, and insects. Frogs live in these freshwater habitats, too. Ponds, lakes, and rivers are not the same habitats as oceans. Do you know why? Salt. Oceans are very

Can you describe this bog turtle's habitat?

salty, and only certain types of animals can live in them. Have you ever tried to drink salt water? Yuck! If you drank a lot, it could make you very sick. And it would do the same thing to animals and plants that like only fresh water.

Many fish live in the ocean. But these fish *like* salt water. What are some other animals that live in the ocean? Clams and oysters do. They have hard shells to protect them from being eaten. Plants such as seaweed live in the ocean, too.

Desert Habitats

The desert is a habitat that has very little water. Many of the animals and plants that live in the desert have developed special ways to live with high temperatures and very little water. Cactuses grow in deserts, and have developed fleshy green stems in which they store water and food. Scorpions rest during the heat of the day and wait until night when it is cool to hunt insects and other small animals. Lizards have scales that help protect them from the hot sun and keep moisture in their bodies. Some lizards get all the water they need from the plants they eat.

Underground Habitats

In the soil, underneath all of the activity on the forest, meadow, and desert floor is a completely different habitat. Can you name some animals that live in the soil? Worms and moles spend most of their time in the soil, except when it rains and they have to scurry from their tunnels. Moles eat worms, along with ants and other insects that make their homes underground. There are some plantlike things called fungi that live in the soil, too. Think about what it must be like to live in such a place! It is very dark all of the time. How would you find food? Moles are nearly blind, but have developed a strong sense of smell and hearing in order to find their food.

Habitat Destruction

So, there are many different kinds of habitats, and many different kinds of animals that have made their homes in each one. Most of these animals have gotten so used to living in one kind of habitat that it would be difficult for them to move to another. They couldn't find the right kind of food, or the right kind of material to make a home or nest, or the right kind of water to drink.

Unfortunately, we humans have begun to crowd other animals out of their homes through habitat destruction. We clear forests for our new houses and office buildings, and we make farms on prairies. We bring water to the desert and make more farms. We fill in ponds with dirt and build our homes on top. We clear and burn the rain forests. What happens to the animals and plants that used to live in these places? They usually die.

Another way we humans have affected other animals' habitats is by polluting the environment. Our smokestacks and cars make the air dirty. We dump trash into lakes, streams, and oceans. Too much of these things make the creatures that live in these habitats very sick, and many of them die.

There is hope that habitat destruction will slow down and the environment will be cleaned up someday, because some people are talking about these problems and looking for solutions.

You can help. Don't leave the faucet running. Turn off lights when you are not using them, to save energy. Help separate your trash so that paper, cans, and bottles can be recycled. These are just a few of the many things you can do to help make the earth a healthier place for all living things.

When you see this on a bottle, box, or can, it means you can recycle.

Special Types of Animals

Pteranodon.

Extinct Animals

Apatosaurus.

Some animals like the dinosaurs used to roam the earth but disappeared. These animals are described as extinct, which means "no longer exist."
No one really knows why the dinosaurs disappeared. They existed a long, long time ago. Traces of dinosaurs have been found all over the world, including the United States! Triceratops, with three horns on its head, lived in

North America, and skeletons of a flying dinosaur, Pteranodon, have been found in Kansas. Some dinosaurs were as tall as houses, so you wouldn't want to get stepped on by one! Many of them ate only plants, but some of them were ferocious meat-eaters. Watch out!

Triceratops.

Wild and Domestic Animals

Animals have always played a very important part in people's lives. Humans used to fear animals like wolves, lions, and bears because people could be eaten by them. But people also killed and ate these animals, and used their skins for clothing.

Things changed when we began to raise sheep, cattle, and other domestic animals. "Domestic" means "of the house," and refers to animals that people raise in or around the house. Domestic animals are wild animals that have been tamed over the years. Cows have become domestic animals.

Pets

Dogs have become domestic too. But instead of using them for food and clothing, we have them as friends or pets. Humans like to have pets. Once we take an animal in to become our pet, we must take good care of it. Our pets depend on us for food, water, and shelter. Pets need a certain amount of play

and exercise to stay healthy. Dogs need a lot more than cats, and cats need a lot more than parakeets.

If you have a pet, you should be aware of these things, and find out what you can do to keep it happy and healthy. Take your dog for a walk every day. Play games with your cat so it can run around. Give your parakeet plenty of room to climb and flap around in its cage.

Make sure you feed your pet the right kind of food for its age, and don't give it too much or too little. Just like a person, it might get too fat or too thin!

A Very Special Animal—You

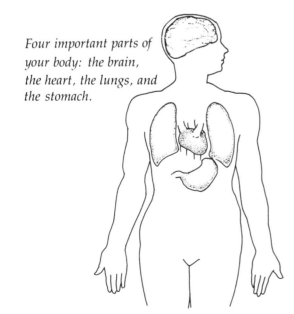

Four important parts of your body: the brain, the heart, the lungs, and the stomach.

Your Body

Have you ever thought about what happens inside your body when you breathe, when you eat, when you run, or when you sleep? Before we go into that, let's start on the outside.

Look at your hand. What is it covered with? Skin. Your skin is a kind of envelope or wrapper for your body, and helps protect it.

Can you name the parts of your body that give it its shape? The bones. They make up your skeleton. They are hard and stiff. But your skeleton can move and bend because the bones have joints, like your elbow or knee. Joints are like hinges on a door; they allow the bones to move while still keeping them together.

Your muscles are wrapped around your bones and are attached to them in several places. Muscles help you run, jump, skip, and lift a pail of water. They even help you talk!

There is one very important muscle that does not help us move. This is the muscle that none of us can do without! Do you know what it is? The heart. Yes, your heart is a muscle, too. The heart is connected to tubes called arteries and veins that go all around your body and back to your heart. Your heart pumps blood to your body through the arteries and veins—a very important job indeed. Have you ever put your hand over your heart after you have been running? Your heart beats faster to get more blood to your muscles and the other parts of your body that are working harder when you run. Put your hand over your heart now. Can you feel it pumping?

Where is the blood going? Well, to many different parts of your body. The blood brings oxygen, an important part of the air we breathe, from your lungs to all the parts of your body. Blood also carries waste away from cells, so they don't get polluted.

See how the muscles of your leg attach to your knee to help it move?

Another part of the body is the stomach. Let's think about our stomach for a minute. Have you eaten recently? If not, you may hear your stomach "growl." If you have, you may hear it making sounds as it digests the food you ate. Your stomach helps break down the food you eat so your cells can use it to do their work.

How does food get to your stomach? The food you eat is first broken into pieces by your teeth when you chew. The watery fluid in your mouth, saliva, helps to digest your food. The work is helped by your senses.

Which of your five senses do you use when you eat? Close your eyes, and let's pretend you see an orange on a table. You look at that orange sitting on the table and you decide you are hungry enough to peel it and eat it. That uses your sense of sight.

You pick up the orange and start to peel it. The peel makes a ripping sound every time you take off a piece. That uses your sense of hearing.

You separate each piece of the orange, and it squirts juice all over your hands. Now you are using your sense of touch.

Then you raise a piece of the orange to your lips and your nose is filled with its strong, sweet aroma. That uses your sense of smell.

You pop that piece of orange into your mouth and WOW! What a sensation! Your whole mouth tingles. That uses your sense of taste. You've used all five senses just by eating an orange!

Now that we've read about some of the parts of the body, and the senses, we should talk about one of the most important parts of all. It's the one that keeps everything working smoothly; it runs the show by sending messages back and forth. Your brain. Your brain connects your sense of smell to your stomach, and starts the digestive process. It connects your sense of sight to your muscles, and helps you catch the ball that's coming toward you. And your brain sends a message to your arm to pull your hand away from a hot iron. Your brain runs so many things that you couldn't function without it.

Taking Care of Your Body

You've probably already figured out that your body is very complicated and amazing. If you take care of it, it will last a lot longer than if you don't. And you will be a lot happier and healthier. You need many of the same things pets need (after all, you are an animal too, remember?): exercise, cleanliness, and the right kinds and amounts of food, plus plenty of rest.

Meat and fish.

Dairy products.

Sometimes, though, you get sick, even though you eat and drink healthy foods like bread, milk, juice, fruit, vegetables, and fish. Your body can't fight off every sickness that comes along.

You might come down with the chicken pox. Chicken pox is a pretty mild disease, but it does cause a slight fever (your body temperature goes up), and small red spots on your skin that are itchy. The mumps, a more serious sickness, causes your neck

Vegetables.

Grains.

to swell up, and you may also have a fever. Measles will make you feverish, and can cause a sore throat. You also develop small red spots on your skin.

Fortunately, scientists have developed shots for some of these diseases. If you get one soon enough, before the disease enters your body, a shot will keep you from getting sick. Even though it hurts a little when you get a shot, the pain goes away pretty fast.

There aren't yet any shots for some diseases, like colds. If you come down with a very bad cold, you might have to go to the doctor and have him or her examine you. Doctors sometimes give out a slip of paper, called a prescription, for a certain kind of medicine. If someone takes this paper to a drugstore, he or she can buy the drug the doctor suggests. These kinds of drugs are very powerful, and therefore can't be sold without a doctor's order. Other kinds of drugs are not so powerful if taken as the package tells you, and can be bought without a prescription. These are called over-the-counter, or nonprescription drugs. Aspirin is a nonprescription drug.

Some drugs are misused by people rather than used as medicine to heal their sickness. These drugs can be very powerful. Drug abusers buy their drugs illegally, from dealers who are breaking the law to sell them. These illegal drugs are very dangerous; they can hurt or kill the person who uses them improperly.

Even aspirin can hurt you if you take too much of it. You must remember never to take any kind of medicine without a grown-up's permission. Also, be careful not to eat or drink things that are lying around. Some of these things may be poisonous and could make you very, very sick, or kill you. Some plants and berries are poisonous. Don't experiment. If you think you have taken too much medicine or have swallowed something poisonous, tell the nearest grown-up right away.

Introduction to Physical Sciences

FOR PARENTS AND TEACHERS

In such physical sciences as chemistry and physics, just as in life sciences, the main teacher of the young child is experience. There is a famous experiment by the Swiss psychologist Piaget which shows that very young children think a tall narrow glass holds more water than a squat thick one, when in fact the glasses hold the same amount. Later on, children do not make this mistake. How have children learned a truer understanding of the physical world? Not from books and science teachers, but from actual experience. Knowledge of physical science must first be "proved upon our pulses," by getting our hands wet and dirty with the size and heft of things, by noticing that when we toss a rock up it falls back down, and by noticing that thunder comes after lightning.

Unfortunately, not all children come to first grade with equal amounts of experience and knowledge of the physical world. One of the main tasks of science teaching in the very early grades is to fill in the important gaps for all children. This must be done systematically in a planned sequence, even if it means going over ground already familiar to some children. For instance, many children will know how to measure the length of something with a ruler. On the other hand they may not know that all measurements have two parts, a number and a measurement unit like an inch, or teaspoon, or hour. Thus, in introducing children to familiar topics in science, there should be something new and interesting for everyone.

The selection and ordering of subjects were decided in exactly the same way as they were in the case of life sciences, described in the little introduction to that chapter. In this chapter, the topics include measurement of length, matter, volume, temperature, and time. Also covered are the shape of the earth and its size, the poles and the equator, the earth's interior, rain, lightning, thunder, and other elements of weather, the moon, the sun as a source of energy, and finally, the nature of experiment.

In dealing with these subjects, we have tried to encourage hands-on experience and experimentation. We describe how to do a few measurements and experiments. But in deference to leaving adults free to decide just how much mess they will tolerate, we have limited the number of specifically suggested experiments. We do urge adults however, to contrive and supervise experiments. We have tried to convey the excitement of scientific discovery, particularly in the final story about Archimedes running naked in the streets shouting, "Eureka! I have found it!" Who knows? You may be nurturing your own young Archimedes or Marie Curie. But at the least you will want to ensure that our children have the basic scientific understanding they need in the modern world.

Physical Sciences

Measurement

Scientists need to measure things. They often need to find out how much of something there is, or how big or little a thing is. Has somebody measured you to see how tall you are? In this section we are going to learn about measuring things.

You know how important it is to measure things if you have ever helped somebody bake a cake. You probably used a recipe that said just what measurements to make. It said measure out a certain amount of this, and a certain amount of that. It said use a pan that measures a certain size. It said set the temperature of the oven, and measure the time the cake should stay in the oven.

There is something wrong with the measurements in this recipe for chocolate cake. Can you figure out what is wrong?

HEALTH & NUTRITION

1 sugar
1½ margarine
½ salt
4 chocolate
1 milk
2 flour

Mix the ingredients together in a bowl, then bake in a pan 12 long and 8 wide at 350 for 45.

Do you see why there's a problem with the recipe? Are we supposed to measure out 1 teaspoon or 1 cup of sugar? Should we bake our cake for 45 seconds or 45 minutes? Is the pan 8 feet or 8 inches wide? The problem is that the recipe doesn't tell us the units to measure with. The recipe has numbers, like 1½ and 350, but it has no units like teaspoons or cups. But you have to say how many units a thing has when you measure it. Saying how many without saying how many whats doesn't let you measure anything at all. Every measurement has a number that says how many followed by a unit that says how many whats.

Let's rewrite the recipe using both numbers and units this time.

1 cup sugar
1½ sticks margarine
½ teaspoon salt
4 ounces chocolate
1 cup milk
2 cups flour

Mix the ingredients together in a bowl, then bake in a pan 12 inches long and 8 inches wide at 350° F for 45 minutes.

There! Each measurement contains a number and a unit, so our recipe is complete. Let the cooking begin!

By making measurements, we can answer questions like "How high can you jump?" "How hot is it outside?" and "How old is your baby sister?" Each measurement includes a number and a unit.

The unit you use for a measurement depends on the things you are measuring. In the chocolate cake recipe, we used cups of milk and teaspoons of salt. It wouldn't make sense to measure milk by minutes. Suppose someone told you to measure three inches of milk. That wouldn't be the right unit, because three inches of milk in a juice cup would be a lot less milk than three inches of milk in a bathtub!

That's enough about measuring for now. You see why you need to have the right units of measurement, and why you have to know how many units there are. Later, we are going to talk about what the different units are, but you can have some fun right now by measuring something. Try this. If you have a spoon and a cup, you can measure how many spoons of water will fill the cup.

Length

How tall are you? Somebody has probably measured your height from head to toe. That means they measured your length. Length is the distance between two places. Your height is the length of your body—the distance from the top of your head to the bottom of your feet.

Lots of times we need to know the length of something. A pilot flying from one city to another needs to know the length (or distance) between the cities so she can put enough fuel in her plane. Better not run out of gas! And it would be hard for a clerk to sell you a pair of shoes if he didn't know the length of your feet.

How do we measure the length of something? One unit of length used long ago was the cubit. This was the distance between the tip of the middle finger and the elbow. Do you know the story of Noah's ark? Noah was supposed to build an ark that was 300 cubits long.

The cubit wasn't a very good way to measure length, though. Some people have longer arms than others, so not all cubits measured the same length. Today, to find out the length of short things, we use measuring sticks with inch or centimeter units marked on them. They are always the same from one ruler to another, not like people's arms.

The distances between the marks on the rulers are used for finding the lengths of very small things. Which is smaller, a centimeter or an inch?

For measuring longer things, like a room, we use feet or meters, because those units are longer. One foot contains 12 inches, and one meter contains 100 centimeters.

How do we measure very long distances, like the distance from New York to California, or from the

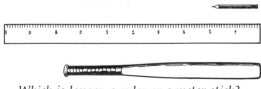

Which is longer, a ruler or a meter stick?

earth to the moon? We could use inches, feet, centimeters, or meters to measure these distances. But it is much easier to use still larger units such as miles or kilometers.

There are 5,280 feet in a mile, and 1,000 meters in a kilometer. And that's a lot.

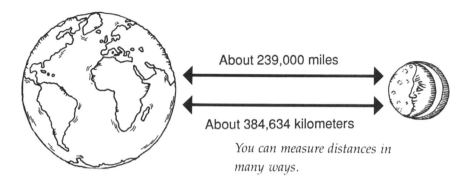

About 239,000 miles

About 384,634 kilometers

You can measure distances in many ways.

Would you use centimeters, meters, or kilometers to measure the length of a tree? What about the length of your foot?

Matter

How are these things alike: an apple, a river, and the air that we breathe? Even though they don't seem the same, they are all made up of matter. Every thing is made of matter. There are three kinds of matter: solid, liquid, and gas. Some matter, like an apple, is solid. The water in a flowing river is liquid. The air we breathe is a gas.

It is easy to see that an apple and a river are things, because we can see and feel them. They are made up of tiny bits of matter called atoms. But how about air? We can't even see air, so how can it be matter? In fact, air is made of atoms, too, but they are so far apart from one another that air is invisible. But you can feel air when the wind blows. The atoms in an apple and a river are closer together, so we can see and feel them more easily. Did you know that atoms are so small that millions of them could fit on top of the period at the end of this sentence. That's pretty small!

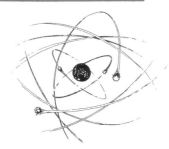

This is a drawing of an atom.

Volume

Volume is the amount of space that a thing fills. A baseball has more volume than a marble does because it takes up more space. Sometimes we need to know just how much volume something has. When we shop for milk, for example, we can buy a quart or a gallon. A gallon of milk contains four times as much milk as a quart.

Here are four quarts and one gallon of milk.

Another unit of volume is a liter. A liter is just a little bit larger than a quart. Soda often comes in one- or two-liter plastic bottles. The volumes of solid things and gases can also be measured in liters and quarts.

Matter usually expands some when it gets hot. This means that its volume gets bigger. Expansion joints, or "cracks," are built into sidewalks so the concrete will have room to expand a little on hot summer days.

> *Can you think of some other things that have volume? After you make a list of these, try to rank them from the smallest to the largest volume.*

There is a famous story from long ago about measuring volume. You can find the story in the last part of this chapter. When you measured how many teaspoons were in a cup, were you measuring volume?

Temperature and Thermometer

Before getting into the bathtub, we usually stick a finger into the water to see whether it is too cold, too hot, or just right. Our fingers tell us something about the temperature of the water. Fingers aren't such good thermometers, though, because some things—like hot ovens—are much too hot to touch. And fingers can't tell the difference between things that have nearly the same temperature. For these reasons, we use a temperature-measuring instrument called a thermometer.

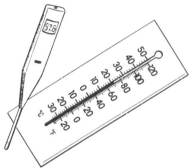

Here are two kinds of thermometers—a digital thermometer and a liquid-in-glass thermometer.

If you have ever been to the doctor's office, you may have used a digital thermometer already. To see if you have a fever, the nurse places the end of the thermometer called the probe under your tongue. The probe sends a message up the thermometer to a window, and a BEEP tells you "Mission accomplished!" Unless you are sick, "98.6°F" appears in the window. That means "ninety-eight-point-six degrees Fahrenheit." Remember, every measurement has a number and a unit. Healthy bodies have a temperature of 98.6 measured in units of degrees Fahrenheit. If you lived in France, your thermometer would read "37°C", because the temperature unit in that part of the world is degrees Celsius or Centigrade. The nurse might say, *"Ta température est normale—trente-sept degrés Celsius. Tu vas bien!"* That means, "Your temperature is normal—thirty-seven degrees Celsius. You are fine!"

Not all thermometers are digital. A liquid-in-glass thermometer is a thin glass tube with a bulb at one end. The bulb holds a colored liquid. On the glass are marks with numbers beside them. You remember that matter expands, or gets larger, when heated. When the bulb is placed under your tongue, your body warms the liquid inside. When warmed, the liquid expands, rising up the tube, and then stops. To read the thermometer you find the number beside the mark that is level with the top of the liquid. This tells you exactly what your temperature is. Where does the liquid stop when you're feeling great? Right beside the "98.6 F" mark.

Are all thermometers just for telling whether we are sick? No. There are weather thermometers to tell us the temperature outdoors, and meat and candy thermometers to help with cooking. They come in different shapes and sizes and may or may not be digital, but they all measure temperature.

With the help of an adult, use a thermometer to take the temperature indoors. Then put the thermometer in a glass of ice water. What happens to the colored liquid? Next, take the thermometer outside and wait until the colored liquid stays in one place. Can you read what the outside temperature is? What happens if you put the thermometer in a sunny spot?

Time

Time tells us how long it takes for something to happen. It also tells us when to do things.

Long ago, people noticed that some things in our world happen over and over again, taking the same amount of time. The sun rises, travels across the sky, and sets. The seasons change from winter to spring to summer to fall, and back to winter again. The rising and setting of the sun and the changing of the seasons have happened over and over again for as long as our earth has been here. People called the amount of time that passes between one sunrise and the next a day, and the amount of time between two winters a year.

Because many of the things that we do—like eating lunch or brushing our teeth—take less time than a day, people divided the day into smaller units of time called seconds, minutes, and hours. "In the wink of an eye" is a saying that means something happens very quickly. It takes about one second to wink your eye. Try it! A second is a very small amount of time. Most things we do take longer than a second. It takes about sixty seconds—or one minute—to wash, rinse, and dry your hands. An hour is an even bigger unit of time. There are sixty minutes in one hour, about the time it takes to bake a cake.

Can you figure out the seasons in these pictures?

We measure time with clocks. Some clocks have faces and hands; others, called digital clocks, have numbers. Here's what they look like:

Clock with hands.

Digital clock.

Seconds, minutes, hours, days, and years are some of the units we use to measure time.

The Earth

We all live on earth, which is a huge ball-shaped object that is surrounded by air. If the earth is round, why doesn't it seem round to us? Because it is so big that we don't even notice that the ground has a curve to it. If the earth were the size of a basketball, the whole city or town that we live in would seem no bigger than a speck of dust.

In earlier times, people thought that the earth was at the center of the universe. These people were so sure of their ideas that they became very angry with scientists who said they were wrong. Today, we are still learning about the earth, the moon, the sun, and the strange and beautiful things our universe contains. But this we know for sure—our world is just one of many specks in space, and not the center of things at all. But because it's our home, it is the center of things for us.

People also used to think that the sun went around the earth once a day. It's easy to see why people thought so. If you have ever gotten up very early in the morning, you may have watched the sun appear down low in the sky. Throughout the day, it seems to travel across the sky, until it sets or disappears just before night. This movement of the sun gave people the idea that the sun was circling the earth. But a man named Copernicus showed that people had things backward. He figured out that the earth spins, or rotates, like a top. The sun doesn't really rise or set at all. It's the spinning of the earth that makes it look that way. Copernicus's explanation is easy to understand if you look straight ahead and spin around very fast. Things seem to move round about you in a circle, but really you are the one doing the moving.

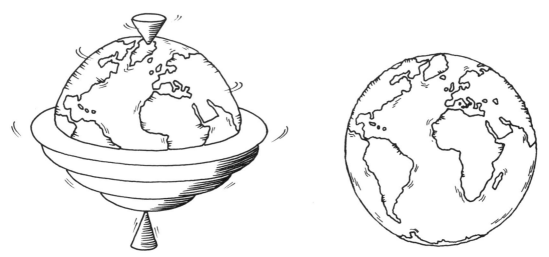

You can imagine the earth spinning like a top.

The Earth's Surface

The earth is bigger than the moon but smaller than the sun. It looks like a ball that is just a little flat at the top and bottom. The top part is called the North Pole, and the bottom part is called the South Pole. Halfway between the North and South Poles is an imaginary circle called the equator, wrapped like a belt around the earth's middle.

A map of the earth shows the Poles and the equator, and a lot more, too. But because maps are flat, they don't show the real shape of the earth at all. A better way to understand the earth is to look at a globe, which is a map shaped like a ball, just like the earth. Both map and globe show Poles, equator, oceans, and continents. Oceans are large bodies of water, and continents are great masses of land. When our earth was very young, there was only one huge continent. Long ago it broke into pieces. If you look at a map, it's not hard to see that the two continents we call South America and Africa used to fit together, just like pieces of a jigsaw puzzle.

Can you find the equator in this picture? Can you find the North and South Poles?

Would you guess there is more land or more water on the earth? A look at a map shows that the earth's surface is mostly water. Notice the color of the

North Pole. It is drawn in white because it is made of ice and snow. Now look at the South Pole, and guess what it is covered with. If you answered "ice and snow," you are exactly right! You may already know that ice is just frozen water. The Poles are made of ice because the light and heat from the sun is weak at the top and bottom parts of the earth. Because the sun shines much more strongly at the equator, the oceans there never get cold enough to freeze.

Inside the Earth

Maps and globes tell us about the earth's surface, but nothing at all about what's underneath. So far, scientists have dug only a short distance below the surface. But what they have found there is pretty amazing—temperatures much too hot for living things. Temperatures high enough to melt rocks!

Because we live on the earth's surface, we don't usually feel this heat. But if you have ever visited a geyser, you have seen signs of the heat inside the earth. A geyser is a jet of hot water and steam that explodes out of a hole in the earth's surface. The steam is water that contains too much heat and energy to exist as a liquid. In the state of Wyoming, there are at least two hundred geysers. The most famous of these shoots a stream of hot water and steam fifty meters into the air—that's taller than most trees. Because this geyser has put on a show for visitors about once an hour for over one hundred years, it is nicknamed "Old Faithful."

What does the geyser "Old Faithful" look like to you?

Weather and the Earth's Atmosphere

My heart leaps up when I behold
A rainbow in the sky . . .

This is the beginning of a famous poem by William Wordsworth. He is explaining how excited he becomes when he sees one of nature's loveliest displays—the rainbow. Rainbows are created when sunlight shines through water droplets. Most people feel the same joy as Wordsworth when they see a rainbow's purples, reds, and yellows. Have you ever seen a rainbow?

Clouds are also made mainly of droplets of water. They are much more common than rainbows, and we see them nearly every day. They may be white or gray, fluffy or thin. The tiny particles of ice and water in clouds sometimes clump together to form drops. When these are big and heavy enough, they fall to the earth as rain. If the temperature is very cold, the water drops freeze into ice as they fall through the air. Then instead of rain we can get sleet or hail. Hailstones sometimes get big enough to put dents in cars and damage roofs. Or we might get snow. Snow is frozen water that falls from clouds to the earth in the form of white, feathery flakes. We use a big word—precipitation—to talk about the water that falls from clouds. Rain, hail, sleet, and snow are all different kinds of precipitation.

Have you ever seen lightning? A lightning bolt is a very long spark between two clouds or between a cloud and the earth. Believe it or not, it is just like the sparks you sometimes see when combing your hair or rubbing your cat in a dark room—only much, much longer. A flash of lightning has so much energy that after we see it we often hear a clap of thunder—BOOM!

Clouds, precipitation, lightning, and thunder—all are found in the air above the earth's surface. We call this air the atmosphere. But what is weather? Well, just look outside your window. Is it cloudy or clear? Rainy or dry? Hot or cold? Windy or calm? When you answer these questions, you have described the weather.

The Moon

When we look up into the sky on a clear night, we can sometimes see the beautiful moon. Even though it seems almost close enough to touch, it is really thousands of miles away.

The moon does not always look the same. Sometimes it seems to be a perfect round disk of light, like a big glowing Frisbee. On other evenings, it seems to have almost disappeared. Why does it look so different at different times?

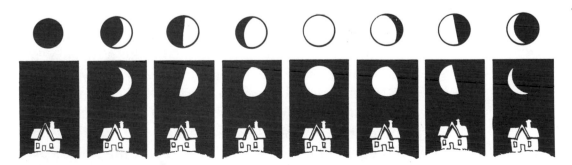

It looks different to us, because it is in a different place in its journey around the earth. The moon travels in a circle around the earth, and completes its trip about once every twenty-seven days. Then it starts all over again. When it is in different parts of its journey, more or less of the moon is lighted by the sun. When it is all lighted to make a full circle, we say it's a "full moon."

The moon is ball-shaped just like earth. But it is much smaller than the earth. It is also not a very friendly place for people to visit. Daytime on the moon is much hotter than any place on the earth, and nights are very, very cold. There are no trees or grass or clouds. There is no water to drink or air to breathe. There are only soil, rocks, and a lot of big holes called craters. No plants or animals live there. Astronauts visiting the moon have to wear spacesuits to give them air to breathe. Neil Armstrong wore such a suit when he was the first man ever to step on the moon in 1969.

Here's "Buzz" Aldrin wearing his spacesuit on the moon.

The Sun and Energy, Part One

When we look around our world, we see grass to walk on and trees to climb. We see fish swimming and hear bees buzzing. Yes, the earth is full of wonderful things. But if it were not for the sun—93 million miles away—our planet would be a cold, dark, unfriendly place. No living things—not even people—could call earth home. How can something so far away be so important to us?

Most of our energy here on earth comes from the sun. But what is energy? How does the sun help the wind blow, the spider spin, and the tractor plow?

Everywhere we look, we see things moving. A kite dances in the wind. A spider spins its web. A tractor plows a field. When things move, they are usually doing work and using energy. Believe it or not, playing hide-and-seek is a lot of work!

Light from the sun helps plants grow. Little bugs that eat these plants get energy from them. Then, the bugs become a meal for the spider, giving it energy to spin its web. The sun also makes kites fly. How? The heat from the sun warms the air near the ground, causing it to expand and rise. Cooler air rushes into the space where the warm air was. This moving air, called wind, makes trees sway and kites dance.

You probably know that the tractor gets energy by burning up fuel. This fuel is what is left of plants and animals that died millions of years ago. Energy from the sun gave those long-ago creatures life.

A thing does not always have to be moving to have energy. Rub your hands together very quickly. How do your palms feel when you stop? Warm! This heat is a kind of energy, too. The energy of your moving hands was changed into heat energy. Can you think of another way to make heat? If you have sat by a fire on a cold winter night, you know that heat can come from a burning log. The energy stored in the wood is changed into heat energy.

Yes, everywhere we look in our world, we see signs of energy—water boiling, snow falling—life changing again and again from one form to another with energy from the sun.

The Sun and Energy, Part Two

The sun is a star, just like the thousands of stars we see when we look into the sky on a dark night. But the sun is very special because it is much closer to us than the other stars. Every animal and plant needs the energy that comes from the sun. The light that we see and the heat that we feel on a bright sunny day is the energy from the sun. It takes about eight minutes for sunlight to make the trip from sun to earth. What a long journey the sun's energy makes to bring life to our planet!

Experiments

Scientists work by doing experiments. But anyone can make experiments. You too can be a scientist whenever you do an experiment that is designed to answer a question you have. Every good experiment tries to answer a question. First, you decide the question you want to ask. Second, you plan an experiment to answer it. Third, you follow your plan, and observe what happens. Fourth, you study what happened to find out whether it really did answer your question.

Suppose we want to answer the question, "Do sunflowers grow better in sunlight or in the dark?" We might guess that the answer is "sunlight," because we have noticed sunflowers growing in bright sunny fields but never in the dark woods. But a guess isn't good enough in science. You have to test your guess with an experiment. So, we buy some sunflower seeds and plant half of them in one container, half in another. After the seeds sprout, we put both containers in a sunny window. But over one of the containers we place a box that lets in air but not light. The other one gets full sunlight from the window. We water the seedlings, and they begin to grow. Each day we observe the sprouts in each container to mea-

sure their height and see how healthy they look. We write down this information in a notebook. After a week or so, we study the observations we wrote
down. Which container's seedlings grew better? Did the amount of sunlight
make a difference? If so, we now have the answer to our question. And that is
the conclusion to our experiment.

One famous experiment took place more than two thousand years ago.
King Hiero II had bought a new crown from a craftsman. The craftsman
claimed that the crown was pure gold, but the King suspected that a cheaper,
lighter metal such as silver had been mixed in. He asked his friend, the
mathematician Archimedes, to find out whether the craftsman was telling the
truth. Archimedes thought long and hard about the problem. Since silver was
lighter than gold, it took more than one cup of silver to weigh the same as one
cup of gold. So if silver was mixed into the crown, it would have more cups of
metal in it than the same weight of pure gold would have. So, Archimedes
said, "I must make an experiment. I must find out whether there are more

cups of metal in the crown than there are in the same
weight of pure gold. But, oh dear, if I melt the crown to
find out how many cups of metal there are, it won't be a
crown any more. The King would be angry. How can I
find out how many cups are in the crown without
melting it?" He had to plan an experiment to find out. It
was hard.

Discouraged, Archimedes decided to take a bath. As
he stepped into his tub, the overflowing water gave him
an idea. He would fill up a bucket full of water. Then he
would put the King's crown into the full bucket, spilling
out water. The number of cupfuls of water that spilled out would be the
number of cupfuls of metal in the crown. Do you see why? Because the
amount of water pushed out by the crown would be the amount of space taken
up by the crown. By using that method, he wouldn't have to melt the crown.
All he had to do was measure the water that spilled out. If the crown pushed
out more water than the same weight of pure gold did, then the crown wasn't
pure gold. But if it pushed out exactly the same amount of water as pure gold
did, then it was pure gold. All he had to do was perform the experiment.

What a great idea! According to the story, Archimedes got so excited about
his plan that he jumped out of the tub, forgetting to dress, and ran naked
down the street shouting "Eureka!" which in Greek means, "I have found it!"

When Archimedes carried out his experiment, he found that the King's crown pushed aside more water than an equal weight of gold did. That meant the gold had been mixed with silver! The craftsman had cheated the King.

Archimedes's experiment seems very different from our experiment with sunlight on flowers. But the two experiments are really a lot alike. In each case, a question was asked. "Will the flowers grow faster with sunlight?" Or "Will the crown push out more water than the same weight of gold?" Then an experiment was planned to find out the answer. It was carried out, and the observations were studied to find out the answer.

Every day, men and women scientists do experiments to help solve some of the questions they want to answer. But it sometimes seems that every answer leads to several new questions. There is always something to do in science. We will never run out of questions, or of people who search for answers.

Stories of Scientists

Nicolaus Copernicus

Today we know the real reason why the sun seems to go around the earth every day. It's because once a day the earth spins around its axis like a spinning basketball. It's the earth that moves, not the sun. But five hundred years ago, people believed that the earth was still and the sun moved around it. Nicolaus Copernicus was brave enough to question that belief. By careful looking and clear thinking he succeeded in discovering the truth that the earth spins, and the sun stands still.

Copernicus was born in Poland in 1473, more than five hundred years ago. After he graduated from a university in Poland, he went to study in Italy. One of the subjects he learned about was astronomy, which is the study of the heavens.

He returned to Poland, and earned money as a clergyman. But in his spare time, he continued to study astronomy and observe the sun and stars. His ideas began to be very different from those he had been taught in school. He came to the conclusion that the earth, not the sun, was moving. He wrote a paper about his ideas, but he didn't have his paper printed up. He was afraid that people would laugh at his "crazy" idea that the sun and stars seem to be moving only because the earth is spinning.

Copernicus's friends began to talk about his new theory. Word spread fast. The Pope in Rome even heard about it. People wanted Copernicus to print his work so that they could read it for themselves. But Copernicus was not ready yet. He knew that rumors of his ideas were making many people very angry. If Copernicus was right, then everybody else's ideas must be wrong!

Although Copernicus didn't share his ideas widely, he kept watching the stars and writing about his findings. He worked with a young astronomer named Rheticus, who was convinced that Copernicus was right. After a time, Rheticus wrote a work explaining Copernicus's theory. Rheticus bravely said: "He who wishes to understand, must have an independent mind." Just a few hours before Copernicus died, he received the first printed copy of the work by Rheticus—the work that gradually made people realize Copernicus was right.

Charles Drew

Charles Drew was born in Washington, D.C., in 1904. In those days, as a black child, he was not allowed to go to the same schools as white children. But he had good schooling with help from his parents, who wanted him to go to college and get a good job. Charles Drew made good grades, because he worked hard at school. He got a scholarship to go to college. He became a star football player and ran on the college track team. Because he wanted to help other people, he decided to become a doctor. In 1928, he entered medical school and began his lifelong scientific study of blood.

Have you had a cut and lost blood? If the cut is very bad you lose cups and cups of blood, and you may need to get more blood to keep you alive. The process of giving you more blood is called a "blood transfusion." Today, this is easy—because of the work of Charles Drew.

It wasn't easy to get a blood transfusion in 1940, when Dr. Drew was working in his laboratory. There was no way to keep blood fresh, or take it where people might need it. Charles Drew discovered that if he got rid of the solid cells in blood, and kept only the liquid part called plasma, the liquid could be stored for a long time. It could be used in transfusions whenever blood was needed. After this discovery, Dr. Drew set up the first blood bank in New York City.

When World War II broke out overseas, many people were wounded and needed blood transfusions. Charles Drew suggested sending plasma instead of whole blood. His idea worked. He started collecting blood, separating the plasma, and shipping it safely to injured people. His work saved thousands of lives.

After America entered World War II, Charles Drew became the first director of the blood bank of the American Red Cross. He went on to lead efforts to collect blood for our country's soldiers and sailors, and for other people too.

For a long time, the Army and Navy refused to accept blood from black people. Even after it started to accept "colored" blood, the Army told the Red Cross to separate the donated blood of black people from that of whites. Charles Drew explained that there was no such thing as "black" and "white" blood. Blood was blood. But no one listened. This made Charles Drew very sad and angry. He resigned from the Red Cross.

Drew began to teach medicine, and became famous as a surgeon. In 1943, he received a special award from the National Association for the Advancement of Colored People (NAACP). By using his talents to help other people, Charles Drew set an example for people of all races. He proved that what you do, not the color of your skin, shows the true worth of a person.

Rachel Carson

When Rachel Carson was growing up on a farm in Pennsylvania, she loved to play in the woods, and observe animals and plants. She started writing when she was young, and often wrote about what she saw in nature.

At college, Rachel decided that she wanted to study animals and plants and to write about them for everybody. But in the days when she was at college, people thought that no one could be both a scientist and a writer. Worse, they thought that no woman could be good at science. Rachel Carson showed these people that they were wrong. She was an excellent writer, and she was good enough at science to earn a master's degree in biology in a time when very few women got master's degrees.

In her first job, Carson worked during the day for the U.S. Government. But late at night, when everyone else was asleep, she wrote about nature. A

magazine editor liked one of her articles about the ocean so much he printed it, and told her she should expand it into a book, which she did.

For the next four years, Carson continued her midnight writing. Her books were a great success, especially one called *The Sea Around Us.* By the 1950s, Rachel had become a full-time writer.

One day, she received a letter from a friend whose property had been sprayed with DDT, a poison designed to kill only bugs. DDT was being used all over the world to help farmers keep bugs from their crops. The letter said that DDT had killed not only bugs but also fourteen robins that lived on the property. The story upset Rachel Carson so much that she began to question scientists about DDT and other poisons that were supposed to be harmless. She found out that these chemicals were hurting animals, soil, and water all over the world!

Carson felt she had to tell people about the danger. But telling the public would make the chemical companies very angry. They had always told the public their poisons were perfectly safe. The government had said the same, so the government might get angry, too.

Rachel Carson bravely decided to tell the public the truth. Her book *Silent Spring* explained that springtime would soon be silent, because there would not be any more birds to sing. They would all be killed by DDT. Because of her book, people began to change their minds about using these chemicals.

Rachel Carson was one of the first to show that the future of all life on earth depends on what we do today. It is up to us to keep the world beautiful and healthy. She said, "Man is a part of nature, and his war against nature is . . . a war against himself."

By her hard work, her courage, and her wonderful writing, Rachel Carson succeeded. *Silent Spring* made people aware of the dangers of certain chemicals. New laws were passed limiting chemical pollution in the United States. Rachel Carson was one of the first heroes in the effort to preserve the natural world around us.

Illustration and Photo Credits

Animals Animals/Breck P. Kent: 203(a)

Animals Animals/Leonard Lee Rue III: 202(a,b), 205(b)

Architect of the Capitol: 116

Australian Overseas Information Services: 99(b)

The Bettmann Archive: 86, 103(c), 109, 119, 128, 131, 145(a,b), 147(a), 150(b), 152, 154(b), 155(a), 156(a,b), 231, 234

Catherine Bricker: 228

Clark Brown: 114

I. Calvino, *Italian Folktales* (Giuniti Publishing Group, 1980): 151(a)

Hancock Shaker Village, Pittsfield, Mass.: 153(d)

Henry Inman, *Se-Quo-Yah*. National Portrait Gallery, Smithsonian Institution, Washington, D.C.: 136

Courtesy of the Library of Congress: 125, 126, 130(a)

Massachusetts Division of Fisheries and Wildlife/Bill Byrne: 124, 198, 203(b), 204(c)

Massachusetts Division of Fisheries and Wildlife/Jack Swedberg: 204(a)

The Massachusetts Historical Society: 127, 132(a,b), 133(a)

The Metropolitan Museum of Art, all rights reserved/Photography by Egyptian Expedition: 101, 153(a)

The Missouri Historical Society, St. Louis: 135(a,b)

Courtesy of Museum of Fine Arts, George Nixon Black Fund, Boston: 130(b)

National Aeronautics and Space Administration: 226(a)

National Museum of the American Indian, Smithsonian Institution: 153(c)

National Park Service: 224

Photo Researchers, Inc./J. Ph. Carbonnier: 91

Photo Researchers, Inc./Mary Evans Picture Library: 229

Photo Researchers, Inc./Carl Frank: 102(a)

Photo Researchers, Inc./National Film Board, Ottawa: 92(c)

Index

Acorns, 204
Activities and resources
  Ancient civilizations, 114
  Animals, 92, 96
  Cave art, 153
  Chinese New Year, 110
  Colonial recipe, 128
  Columbus coloring
    book/panorama, 118
  Continents, 96
  Fairy-tale books, in library,
    56
  Indian books, 123
  Indian recipe, 124
  Metric length, 217
  Months of the year, rhyme
    for, 187
  Picture journal, 135
  Portrait/self-portrait, 155
  Pyramids, 104, 156
  Sayings, 81
  Sphinx, 156
  Symmetrical picture, 154
  Temperature, 220
  "Three Bears,"
    dramatization of, 32
  Volume, 218
Adams, Abigail, 132
Adams, John, 132
Addition, 163–68, 173–74,
  178, 187–91
Aesop's Fables. See Fables
Africa, 84–85, 91–92, 112,
  126–27, 150, 152, 153
Alaska, 112
Aldrin, Buzz, 226
Allah, 107
Alphabet, 71–72
Alps, 90
A.M., 78, 184

Amazon River, 95
American civilization, 111–
  136
American Indians. See
  Native Americans
American Red Cross, 233
"America the Beautiful," 148–
  49
"Anansi Rides Tiger," 15,
  27–28
Andes Mountains, 95, 116
Animal gods, 104
Animals, 89, 90, 91, 92, 94,
  96, 198, 201–2
  Domestic, 207–8
  Eating habits, 201
  Extinct, 207
  Habitats of, 203–6
  Wild, 207
Antarctica, 95–96
Apostrophe, 74
"Apple a day keeps the
  doctor away, An," 78
"April showers bring May
  flowers," 79
Arabia, 107
Archimedes, 213, 229–30
Architecture, 139, 155–156
Arithmetic, 160–79
Armstrong, Louis, 147
Armstrong, Neil, 226
Art, visual, 152–56
Asia, 84–85, 89, 90, 106–107,
  112
Astronauts, 226
Astronomy, 231
Atlantic Ocean, 80, 90, 94
Atmosphere, 224–225
Atoms, 217–18
Australia, 96

Aztecs, 115, 119, 120

"Baa, Baa, Black Sheep," 17
Babylon, 98, 105
Ballet, 151
Bears, 92, 94, 201, 202, 203, 207
Blood, 209, 232–33
    Blood bank, 233
    Transfusion, 232–33
Body. *See* Human body
Bones, 208–9
Boone, Daniel, 126
Boston, 123, 124, 127
Boston Tea Party, 127
"Boy Who Cried Wolf, The," 59
Brahma, 107
Brain, 210
"Brer Rabbit and the Tar Baby, The Fable of," 68–69
Buddha/Buddhism, 107–8
Buffalo, 94

Cactuses, 205
Calculators, 178–79
Calendar, 186–87
Camel, 91
Canada, 93
Capital letters, 72
Carson, Rachel, 233–35
Celsius, 219
Centimeter, 216–17
Central America, 95, 114
Characters, in stories, 76
Cherokee Indians, 136
"Chicken Little," 28–29
Chicken pox, 210
China, 89, 108–9
Chinese New Year, 109, 110
Christianity, 106
"Cinderella," 16, 29–30, 64
Circle, 180
Clams, 205
Classical music, 144–46

Clocks, 183–185
Clouds, 224–25
Colonies, 121–29
Columbus, Christopher, 116–18
Comma, 74
Confucius, 108
Consonants, 71
Continents, 89–96
Contraction, 74
Copernicus, Nicolaus, 222, 231–32
Cornet, 147
Cortés, Hernando, 119
Counting
    Money, 191–93
    to 100, 178
Cows, 201, 207
Crescent, 106
Cross, 106
Cube, 181
Cubit, 216

Daedalus, 67–68
Dance, 139, 150–52
    Ballet, 151
    Folk, 151
    Tap, 152
Dare, Virginia, 122
Da Vinci, Leonardo, 155
Day, 220–21
Days in a week, 186
DDT, 234
Deciduous plants, 200
Declaration of Independence, 130–31
Desert, 91
Desert habitat, 205
"Diddle, Diddle, Dumpling," 17
Digestion, 209–10
"Diller, a Dollar, A," 14, 17
Dinosaurs, 207
Diseases, 118, 119, 210–11
    Chicken pox, 210
    Measles, 211

Mumps, 210–11
Smallpox, 118, 119
Dixieland Jazz, 147
"Dog in the Manger, The,"
60
Dogs, 207–8
"Do unto others as you
would have them do
unto you," 79
"Down in the Valley," 143
Drawing, 152
Drew, Charles, 232–33
Drugs, 211

"Early to Bed," 14, 17
Earth, 86–87, 221–25, 231
Atmosphere, 224–25
Interior, 223–24
Surface, 222–23
Egypt, 98, 99–104, 156
Elephant, 201
Elves, 64
Empire State Building, 155
Energy, 226–28
England, 120–22, 127
Equals sign, 164
Equator, 88–89, 222–23
Eskimos, 155
Europe, 90
Evergreen, 200
Exclamation point, 73, 74
Experiments, 228–30

Fables, 58–63, 68–69
Fact families, 173–74
Fahrenheit, 219
Fairies, 64
Fairy tales, 16
Familiar rhymes, 16–26
Ferdinand, King, 117
Figures, open and closed,
181
Fish, 204–5
"Fish out of water," 79
Florida, 136
Flowers, 200

Folk dancing, 151
Food chain, 202–3
Forest habitat, 204
1492, 118
"Fox and the Grapes, The,"
62
Fractions, 182–83
Franklin, Benjamin, 128
Freeman, Elizabeth, 132
Freshwater habitat, 204–5
Frogs, 204
Fuel, 227
Fungi, 206

Gallon, 218
Gas, 217
Geography, 84–96
Geometry, 179–81
"Georgie Porgie," 18
Geyser, 224
Glacier, 93
Globe, 222
God(s), 104–7
"Goldilocks and the Three
Bears," 31–32
"Goose and the Golden
Eggs, The," 63
Greater than (>), 168–69
Guatemala, 94
Guitar, 142, 150

Habitats, 203–6
Air and treetop, 203
Desert, 205
Destruction of, 206
Forest, 204
Meadow and prairie, 204
Underground, 205–6
Water, 204–5
Hail, 225
Hammurabi, 105
"Hare and the Tortoise,
The," 62–63
Harmony, 147, 150
Heart, 209

"Here We Go Round the
    Mulberry Bush," 19, 141
Heroes and heroines, 76
"Hey, Diddle, Diddle," 18,
    75
"Hickory, Dickory, Dock," 18
Hinduism, 107
History, 99
"Hit the nail on the head,"
    79
"Hot Cross Buns!" 18
Hours, 183–85, 220
Human body, 208–11
    Arteries and veins, 209
    Blood, 209
    Brain, 210
    Heart, 209
    Muscles, 209
    Skeleton, 208–9
    Skin, 208
    Stomach, 209
    Taking care of, 210–11
"Humpty Dumpty," 14, 19
"Hush, Little Baby," 141

Icarus, 68
"If at first you don't succeed,
    try, try again," 80
Igloos, 155
Incas, 116, 119, 120
Inch, 216–17
India, 89, 107
Indians, American. *See*
    Native Americans
Isabella, Queen, 117
Islam, 107
Israel, 105
"I've Been Working on the
    Railroad," 144

"Jack and Jill," 18
"Jack and the Beanstalk," 32–
    34
"Jack Be Nimble," 19
"Jack Sprat," 17
Jaguar, 94

Jamestown, 122–23, 136
Jazz, 146–47
Jefferson, Thomas, 130–31,
    134–35
Jesus, 106
Judaism, 105
July 4, 1776, 130

Kangaroo, 96
Kilometer, 217
Koala bear, 96
Koran, 107

Labyrinth, 67–68
"Ladybug, Ladybug," 17
Land. *See* Continents
Language, 70–74
Legends, 64, 66–68
Length, 216–17
Leprechaun, 64
Less than (<), 169
Letters, 71–73
"Let the cat out of the bag,"
    80
Lewis and Clark, 134–35
Liberty Bell, 131
Life sciences, 196–211
Lightning, 225
Lions, 207
Liquid, 217
Liter, 218
Literature, 70, 75–76, 139
"Little Bo Peep," 21
"Little Boy Blue," 19
"Little Jack Horner," 21
"Little Miss Muffet," 20
"Little Red Hen, The," 34–35
"Little Red Riding Hood,"
    16, 35–36
Lizards, 205
"London Bridge Is Falling
    Down," 19, 140
Louisiana Purchase, 134–35,
    136
Lowercase letters, 72

Magic Flute, The, 146
"Maid and the Milk Pail, The," 61
Map(s)
    Africa, 90, 100
    American colonies, 121
    Asia, 90, 100
    Atlantic Ocean, 88, 90, 93
    Europe, 90, 100
    How to read, 87
    Louisiana Purchase, 134
    North and South America, 93, 113
    Pacific Ocean, 88, 90, 93
    United States, 134
    World, 88
"Mary, Mary, Quite Contrary," 20
"Mary Had a Little Lamb," 20
Massachusetts, 129
Massachusetts Bay Colony, 124
Mathematics, 158–94
Matter, 217–18
Maya, 114
Mayflower, 124
Maze, 67–68
Measles, 211
Measurement, 214–17, 218–21
"Medio Pollito," 15, 37–38
Mediterranean Sea, 90
Melody, 147–49
Melville, Herman, 97
Meter, 216, 217
Mexico, 94–95, 115, 120
Mile, 217
Minerals, 198
Minos, King, 67–68
Minotaur, 67
Minus sign (−), 170
Minutemen, 129
Mississippi River, 94, 134
Mohammed, 107
Moles, 205–6

Mona Lisa, 155
Money, 191–93
Months in a year, 186–87
Moon, 225–26
"More the merrier, The," 80
Moses, 105
Mother Goose, 16
Mountains
    Alps, 90
    Andes, 95, 116
    Ural, 90
Mozart, 144–46
Mummies, 98, 103
Mumps, 210–11
Muscles, 209
Music, 139, 140–50
    Classical, 144–46
    Folk, 143–44
    Instrumental, 142
    Jazz, 146–47
    Opera, 146
    Vocal, 142
Myths, 64, 66–68

NAACP, 233
Native Americans, 117–18, 120, 121, 122–23, 135–36, 153, 155
    Cherokee, 136
"Never leave till tomorrow what you can do today," 80
New Orleans, 134
Nile River, 91, 99–102
Niña, 117
North America, 92–95, 112
North Pole, 222, 223
Numbers
    Ordinal, 175
    0 to 10, 161–63
    See also Arithmetic
Nursery rhymes, 16–26

Oceans, 88, 222, 223
    Atlantic, 88, 90, 94

Pacific, 88, 89, 94, 96, 116
Oedipus, 66–67
"Oh, Susanna!" 148
"Old Faithful," 224
"Old King Cole," 16, 20
"Old Mother Hubbard," 23
"One, Two, Buckle My
    Shoe," 16, 21
Opera, 146
Orchestra, 146, 151
Ordinal numbers, 175
"Owl and the Pussycat,
    The," 22
Oysters, 205

Pacific Ocean. *See* Oceans,
    Pacific
Painting, 139, 152, 154–55
Panda, 89
Paragraphs, 73
Parakeet, 208
Parentheses, 74
Passover, 105
"Pat-a-Cake," 21, 149
Penguin, 96
Period, 74
"Peter Rabbit," 38–39
Pets, 207–8
Philadelphia, 131
Physical sciences, 212–230
Piaget, Jean, 212
Piano, 142, 150
"Pied Piper of Hamelin,
    The," 40–41
Pilgrims, 123–24
Pine tree, 200
"Pinocchio," 42–43
Pinta, 117
Pizarro, Francisco, 119
Place value, 175–78
Plantations, 127
Plants, 198–201, 203–6
    Deciduous, 200
    Evergreen, 200
Plasma, 232–33
Plural, 73

Plus sign (+), 164
P.M., 78, 184
Pocahontas, 122–23
Polar bear, 92
Pollution, 206, 234
Portraits, 154–55
Powhatan, 122–23
"Practice makes perfect," 81
Prairie dogs, 204
Prescription, 211
"Princess and the Pea, The,"
    43–44
Prose, 75
Punctuation marks, 73–74
Puritans, 124–25
"Puss-in-Boots," 44–46
Pyramids, 98, 102, 103–4,
    114, 156

Quart, 218
Question mark, 73, 74

Raccoons, 204
Rain, 224–25
"Rain, Rain, Go Away," 24
Rainbows, 224
"Raining cats and dogs," 81
Raleigh, Sir Walter, 121–22
"Rapunzel," 46–47
Recipes
    Chocolate cake, 214–16
    Colonial, 128
    Indian, 124
Rectangle, 179
Revere, Paul, 129
Revolution, American. *See*
    Revolutionary War
Revolutionary War, 127–29,
    132, 133
Rhyme, 75
Rhymes, 14–26
Rhythm, 147, 149–50
"Ride a Cock-horse," 23
"Ring Around the Rosey,"
    16, 21

Rivers
  Amazon, 95
  Mississippi, 94, 134
  Nile, 91, 99–102
  Yellow, 108
"Rock-a-bye, Baby," 23
Roots, 199–200
"Roses Are Red," 24
"Row, Row, Row Your Boat,"
  140
"Rub-a-dub-dub," 24
"Rumpelstiltskin," 48–49

Sacajawea, 135
Sahara Desert, 91–92
St. Augustine, 136
Sampson, Deborah, 132
Santa Maria, 117
"Satchmo" (Armstrong,
  Louis), 147
Sayings, 77–81
Scientists, biographies of,
  231–34
Scorpions, 205
Sculpture, 139, 153, 155–56
Seaweed, 205
Seeds, 199–201
"See-Saw, Margery Daw," 23
Senses, 209–10
Sentences, 73
Sequoyah, 136
Shaker art, 153–54
Shapes, 179–81
  Flat, 179–80
  Solid, 181
Sheep, 207
Shots, 211
Silent Spring (Rachel Carson),
  233–35
"Simple Simon," 25
"Sing a Song of Sixpence,"
  14, 24
Singular, 73
Skeleton, 208–9
Skin, 208
Slavery, 126–127

"Sleeping Beauty," 50–51
Sleet, 225
Smallpox, 118, 119
Smith, John, 122–23
Snails, 204
Snow, 225
"Snow White," 52–54
Solid (matter), 217
Solid shapes, 181
Songs, 140–46, 148–49
Sour grapes, 62
South America, 95, 116
South Pole, 222, 223
Soviet Union, 89
Spain, 117, 118, 119, 120, 136
Sphere, 181
Sphinx (creature), 66–67
Sphinx (statue), 104, 156
Square, 180
Square dancing, 151
Squirrels, 204
Star, 228
"Star Light, Star Bright," 23
Star of David, 105
"Star-Spangled Banner,
  The," 140, 142
States, 94
Statue of Liberty, 156
Statues. *See* Sculpture
Stomach, 209
Stories, 16, 27–57, 65–66
Subtraction, 170–74, 187–91
Sun, 226–28, 231
Sunflower experiment, 228–
  29
Symmetry in art, 153–54
Symphony, 146

Tap dancing, 152
Teepees, 155
Temperature, 219–20
"There's no place like home,"
  81
"There Was a Little Girl," 25
"There Was an Old Woman
  Who Lived in a Shoe," 26

Thermometer, types of, 219, 220
"Thirty Days Hath September," 187
"This Little Pig Went to Market," 14, 26
Thor, 64
"Three Billy Goats Gruff, The," 65–66
"Three Blind Mice," 14, 25
"Three Little Pigs, The," 54–55
Thunder, 225
Time, 78, 183–85, 220–21
    Digital clock, 185, 221
    Face clock, 183–85, 221
"Tom, Tom, the Piper's Son," 23
Tree, parts of, 199–200
    Evergreen, 200
Triangle, 179–80
Troll, 64–66
Tutankhamen, King, 99–104
"Twinkle, Twinkle, Little Star" 25, 145

"Ugly Duckling, The," 55–56
United States, 94, 130, 134
Uppercase letters, 72

Ural Mountains, 90

Virginia, 122, 129
Volcanos, 92
Volume, 218
Vowels, 71

Washington, George, 133
Washington, D.C., 94, 133
Water habitat, 204–5
Weather, 224–25
Wheatley, Phillis, 132
"When the Saints Go Marching In," 146
Whistler, James, 154
"Why the Owl Has Big Eyes," 15, 56–57
Wildflowers, 204
"Wolf in Sheep's Clothing, The," 60–61
Wolves, 94, 207
Words, 71–73
Wordsworth, William, 224
World civilization, 97–110

"Yankee Doodle," 141
Year, 220, 221
Yellow River, 108

Zero, 162, 165

COLLECT THE ENTIRE CORE KNOWLEDGE SERIES

ISBN	TITLE	PRICE
41115-4	What Your 1st Grader Needs To Know	$22.50/$28.00Can
41116-2	What Your 2nd Grader Needs To Know	$22.50/$28.00Can
41117-0	What Your 3rd Grader Needs To Know	$22.50/$28.50Can
41118-9	What Your 4th Grader Needs To Know	$22.50/$28.00Can
41119-7	What Your 5th Grader Needs To Know	$22.50/$28.00Can
41120-0	What Your 6th Grader Needs To Know	$22.50/$28.00Can

READERS:

The titles listed above are available in your local bookstore. If you are interested in mail ordering any of the Core Knowledge books listed above, please send a check or money order only to the address below (no C.O.D.s or cash) and indicate the title and ISBN book number with your order. Make check payable to Doubleday Consumer Services (include $2.50 for postage and handling). Allow 4–6 weeks for delivery. Prices and availability subject to change without notice.

Please mail your order and check to:
Doubleday Consumer Services, Dept. CK
2451 South Wolf Road
Des Plaines, IL 60018

EDUCATORS AND LIBRARIANS:

For bulk sales or course adoptions, contact the Bantam Doubleday Dell Education and Library Department. Outside New York State call toll-free 1-800-223-6834 ext. 9238. In New York State call 212-492-9238.

FOR MORE INFORMATION ABOUT CORE KNOWLEDGE:

Call the Core Knowledge Foundation at 1-800-238-3233.